Higher French Course Notes

Brian Templeton, Lisa Albarracin
and Betty Templeton

Leckie ✕ Leckie

Scotland's leading educational publishers

Text © 2004 Brian Templeton, Lisa Albarracin and Betty Templeton
Design and layout © 2004 Leckie & Leckie
Cover Image © Corbis

09/091009

ISBN 978-1-84372-081-2

Published by
Leckie & Leckie Ltd, 4 Queen Street, Edinburgh EH2 1JE
Tel: 0131 220 6831 Fax: 0131 225 9987
enquiries@leckieandleckie.co.uk www.leckieandleckie.co.uk

Edited by Dorothy Drylie and Sandrine Jambert

Special thanks to
Mark DiMeo (illustration), BRW (creative packaging), Pumpkin House (concept design),
Phil Booth (sound engineering) and the French speakers: Christian Baudot, Anabelle Bergès,
Marie-Alix Cuttier, Pascal Faurie and Danielle Gera.

A CIP Catalogue record for this book is available from the British Library.

Leckie & Leckie makes every effort to ensure that all paper used in our books is made from wood pulp obtained from well-managed forests, controlled sources and recycled wood or fibre.

Leckie & Leckie is a division of Huveaux plc.

Contents

Section 1: Introduction

Purpose and Content

Some Thoughts on Learning a Foreign Language

Content of the Higher Teaching and Assessment Syllabus

Introduction to the Practice Activities

Introduction

Purpose and Content

This book is produced primarily as a study aid for students preparing for the Higher French examination but will also be of interest to teachers. Consequently, the book is written in a relatively informal style similar to that used between teacher and student working together at Higher Level. The book has been written by two practising teachers and the Principal Assessor for French in order to highlight the key areas of language learning that students and teachers should concentrate on in preparation for the demands of the external exam. The book concentrates on developing the four language skills (speaking/listening/reading/writing) within the most productive themes and topics and also explains how each skill is assessed in the external examination.

For the Student

This book is intended to support, not to replace, the teaching programme that you will have been following. The book is designed to help you:

- to understand the requirements of the Higher French Exam
- to practise and develop your ability and confidence in speaking, listening, reading and writing
- to ensure that you are fully prepared to give your best performance in all parts of the final exam.

The aim throughout is to concentrate on the key language and structures required at Higher Level and the book provides activities and resources which allow you to practise this new language so that you can use it with confidence and accuracy. To enable you to check how well you are doing, all the exercises in the main book have answers provided in the pocket section.

For the Teacher

This book can be used to complement and enhance any teaching programme built around a course book or Higher Still support materials. It does not replicate texts nor the teaching style which is incorporated in the Higher Still support materials but rather concentrates on developing the key language skills within the most productive topic areas. The book fills a significant gap in the support materials by providing activities which encourage the student to practise at length (but in a variety of ways) the key language they need in order to do well in the external exam. In particular, the provision of short, targeted listening activities develops not only comprehension of the key language but provides a model for the student to practise the correct pronunciation.

This teaching resource can form the basis of class work with pupils and then be the basis for independent practice as homework.

Some Thoughts on Learning a Foreign Language

Firstly the good news

By the time you are sitting Higher French you will already have mastered at least one language to a high level, namely your own language, probably English. In doing so you will have developed your ability in English partly by being immersed in it and partly by studying it formally at school, where you will have developed skills in speaking, listening, reading and writing and will have discussed many of the grammar rules which help English operate as a language system. These are all skills that you can draw upon when you are learning French. Also by the time you are studying Higher French you will probably have studied French for at least four years previously in the secondary school. So, you should be starting your Higher French teaching programme with a lot of knowledge in English on which to draw and you will have at your disposal a lot of knowledge of French. As you begin to work towards the Higher examination, you need to make maximum use of what you already know in French and in English in order to develop your language skills to a 'Higher Level'.

The bad news

You don't have the same amount of time to learn French that you had to learn your own native language of English. Therefore, you will have to speed up the process and that means you have to learn vocabulary rather than just pick it up naturally and also you need to understand the key grammar rules and learn and practise these more formally than you did when you picked up your own language.

The really good news

This book provides you with the essential new vocabulary at Higher Level and provides activities that help make vocabulary learning less of a grind. The book also explains and practises grammar points only when they are essential to the context.

Content of the Higher Teaching and Assessment Syllabus

The good news

There are only three prescribed themes: Lifestyles, Education and Work, and the Wider World, and these subdivide into six topic areas. These will be the topics you will study in depth with your teacher and they are the same topics which the examiners will use to test you in the final examination. So, if you are well prepared on these themes and topics, there should be no (or at least very few) nasty surprises waiting for you in the final exams. The message to remember is that if you work hard in preparation, the exams should allow you to demonstrate what you have learned and to reproduce the best level of performance of which you are capable in each of the four language skills: speaking, listening, reading and writing.

The bad news

There is still a lot of content to cover in the time available and you will be expected to deal with this content at a high level of ability. You won't be able to develop all the topics to the same level and you (and your teacher) will have to be selective in what aspects of the topics you really concentrate on and then practise.

The really good news

This book has already done the selection for you and concentrates only on the topics that are likely to be of most interest to you and which are most likely to be chosen as the content of the external exam. For this reason the book incorporates aspects of the Wider World (Ideal Holidays/Holidays With or Without Parents) into the theme of Lifestyles in order to create one main theme, which in itself will leave students well prepared for Speaking, Listening and Writing.

So let's look at each of the themes and topics in more detail so that you first fully understand how these topics should be dealt with at Higher Level!

Lifestyles:

This is the theme you will probably spend most time on and it subdivides into two very important topics:

1   Family, Friends and Society

2   Leisure and Healthy Living

'But I've done Family, Friends and Leisure for years, so what's the difference at Higher Level?'

That's an important question and you need to be absolutely clear about the answer before you begin to learn the French you need for the Higher exam. So, what **is** the difference when dealing with these topics at **Higher Level?**

When speaking, listening, reading and writing on these topics at Higher Level, **the content** will deal with issues, ideas and opinions and **the language** you use in French will be more complex and advanced (and hopefully more grammatically accurate).

These differences can be seen most clearly, when you consider how you will speak about these topics at Higher Level. The level of discussion will require you to express ideas and opinions giving reasons for and against. It will require you to express not only your own ideas and opinions on the topics but to understand the views and opinions held by others (**Society**) and you will be expected to agree or disagree with those views. The higher level of language will require you to have a greater variety of ways of expressing your ideas and opinions and a greater grammatical accuracy allowing you to develop longer and more complex sentences.

Let's look for example at Family, Friends and Society!

In this topic, you will already be familiar with a lot of relevant vocabulary and you will probably be able to give factual information and physical descriptions of your family and friends. However, at Higher Level, you will be expected to develop this topic in order to discuss issues such as your relationship with your brothers, sisters and parents and any causes of conflict. You might also discuss the amount of independence you are given by your parents or the qualities you look for in a friend. You might revisit the topic of 'home area' where previously you will have learned how to describe what buildings there are and what there is to do in your area. Now you'll be expected to highlight the advantages and disadvantages of your home area and the facilities that are available for people of your age. You may also be asked to give your opinion on the advantages or disadvantages of living in a town as opposed to the countryside.

At Higher Level, 'Leisure' is now linked to 'Healthy Living', so you will be expected to go beyond saying **what** you do in your leisure time to discuss **why** you do it. You will need to consider how important to you are sport, diet and a healthy lifestyle and be able to discuss views, held by you and by others, on smoking and drinking.

Education and Work:

Topic 1:   School/College

Topic 2:   Careers

Again you will know a lot of vocabulary particularly related to school and should be able to say which subjects you study, when they appear on your timetable and why you like some subjects more than others. At Higher Level, you will be expected to discuss what makes a good school or a good teacher and to comment on the range of subjects and extra-curricular activities offered by your school. You will be expected to be aware of the situation in French schools and should be able to make some comparisons between French and Scottish schools. You might also be expected to discuss the issue of school uniform, its advantages and disadvantages. You will be required to outline in French your own personal record of achievement to date in terms of subjects studied, experience gained and to develop this into your future career aspirations. This may involve you in discussing plans to study further at university and a discussion of what is important for you in a career. As you have chosen to study French, you should be able to discuss the value and importance of learning a foreign language!

The Wider World:

Topic 1: Holidays and Travel

Topic 2: Tourism

Again you will have a lot of vocabulary on which you can draw and again the progression is from saying where and how you travel to the reasons why you choose that sort of transport or prefer that holiday destination. You might also wish to discuss what's important to you in a holiday and whether you prefer to holiday with friends of your own age or with your parents, and again what the advantages and disadvantages of either type of holiday would be. In the topic of Tourism, you can again develop your own home area but this time concentrating on the advantages or disadvantages of it from a tourist perspective. You will also be expected to have an awareness of places of interest to tourists in French speaking countries.

Okay! Now you should be clear as to what **content** you have to cover and what will be expected in terms of the way you discuss these topics. Let's now look at how we can practise and prepare for the final exam.

Introduction to the Practice Activities

The activities that follow give practice in developing the four language skills within the topic development strand, which are most popular both with students and examiners. Each topic development strand is developed in the following way:

- Students are **reminded** of how this topic should be developed at Higher Level.
- Students are **introduced** to the key language used in this topic and given activities to help them learn this vocabulary.
- Students **listen** to a native speaker of French using the key language and **demonstrate** understanding of it.

- Students **listen** again while **studying** the transcript of the recording in order to ensure accurate comprehension of what is said.
- Students **practise** pronunciation of the new language after **listening** to the recording.
- Students **study** the language in written form and **demonstrate** comprehension and/or **translate** accurately into English (answers to all the translations are provided in the answer section).
- Students **select** the key language appropriate to their own situation and **practise** it in spoken and written form.

Some points to note:

Learning Vocabulary

The following sections concentrate on the essential vocabulary needed to develop each of the topic areas at Higher Level. However, you will already know a lot of vocabulary related to these topic areas and you will have other lists of vocabulary that you will need to learn. When learning vocabulary, you need to distinguish between **words that are so important that you need to memorise them** so that you can write them accurately and other **words that you simply need to recognise and understand**. The following activities give practice of both types of vocabulary learning through timing games and this approach can be extended to the revision of previously learned vocabulary relevant to the topic areas. Remember, although you can use a dictionary in most parts of the exam, you won't have time to look up every word and the dictionary is no substitute for learning important words off by heart.

Grammar

At Higher Level, you will need to understand the key rules of the grammar system so that you can understand and translate accurately what you listen to and read. You will also need to be able to apply these rules in order to speak and write as accurately as possible. The following activities do not contain detailed notes on grammar rules but rather highlight and practise specific aspects of grammar as they are used in the various topics, e.g. agreement of adjectives when discussing qualities of friends/ideal parents.

As grammar will help with the structure of your sentences and your understanding of a language, you really should try to ensure that you know the grammatical structures quite well.

Here is a checklist of the main grammar points that you should really know at Higher Level.

Tick them off once you are happy that you know each structure.

GRAMMAR POINTS Tenses (both regular and irregular verbs)

Present tense	e.g. je fais, je vais
Perfect tense	e.g. j'ai fait, je suis allé(e)
Pluperfect tense	e.g. j'avais fait, j'étais allé(e)
Imperfect tense	e.g. je faisais, j'allais
Future tense	e.g. je ferai, je vais faire
Conditional tense	e.g. je ferais, j'irais
Modal verbs	e.g. vouloir, devoir, falloir, pouvoir, etc.
Reflexive verbs	e.g. se lever, se coucher, etc.
Negatives	e.g. ne … pas, ne … rien, ne … que
Adjective agreements	e.g. une belle femme, une grande table
Possessive adjectives	e.g. mon, ma mes, ton, ta tes
Comparatives	e.g. plus grand que, moins belle que
Superlatives	e.g. le/la/les plus grand(e,s)
Personal pronouns	e.g. je, tu, il, elle, lui, moi, etc.
Position of pronouns	e.g. il m'a aidé
Prepositions (position)	e.g. devant, derrière, en face de, etc.

Section 2: Practice Activities

Theme 1 – Lifestyles and The Wider World

Theme 2 – Education and Work

Directed Writing

TOPIC 1 Family, Friends and Relationships – La Famille, Les Amis et Les Relations

We shall begin by looking at the first theme in the Higher programme. Lifestyles.

Let's start by brainstorming some of the ideas we will wish to discuss! Here are a few ideas but feel free to add any others you can think of.

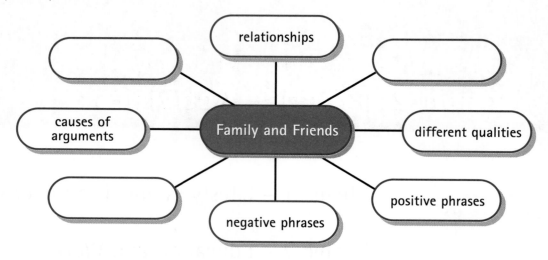

Although you will already know a lot of vocabulary to help you talk about relationships, here is a little reminder of some of the most important phrases.

General vocabulary

- faire partie d'une famille nombreuse — *to be part of a large family*
- un frère aîné/cadet — *older/younger brother*
- une sœur aînée/cadette — *older/younger sister*
- avoir un bon/mauvais rapport avec quelqu'un — *to have a good/bad relationship with someone*
- les rapports familiaux — *family relationships*
- faire confiance à quelqu'un — *to trust someone*
- bien s'entendre avec quelqu'un — *to get on with someone*
- se sentir proche de quelqu'un — *to feel close to someone*
- se confier à quelqu'un — *to confide in someone*

We will now look at the last four in a little more detail.

On the CD you will hear each of these four phrases in the infinitive form with an example in the Present Tense as shown below.

To help prepare you for your talk, practise the pronunciation of each phrase and example along with the CD.

Faire confiance à quelqu'un
exemple, Je fais confiance à ma sœur aînée.

Bien s'entendre avec quelqu'un
exemple, Je m'entends bien avec mes parents.

Se sentir proche de quelqu'un
exemple, Je me sens proche de mon frère cadet.

Se confier à quelqu'un
exemple, Je me confie toujours à ma meilleure amie.

Exercise 1 – If you want to practise your translation skills you can try translating the above sentences into English.

TRACK 1

Exercise 2a – You will now hear four sentences three times. Each sentence contains one of the verb phrases on the previous page.

Listen to each sentence and try to write down exactly what you hear. Think about the spelling of the French words. Bonne chance!

Bravo! Tu as réussi!

Now look at Transcript 2 to check your answers.

You may find that you have misspelled some of the words. If so, listen to the CD again reading the transcript at the same time to see where you have made the mistakes.

Write a list of any problem words and practise the pronunciation of these words, using the CD to help you.

Exercise 2b – You may wish to translate these sentences into English.

Here are some important adjectives that you may wish to revise! How well do you really know them?

Positive		Negative	
abordable	– *approachable*	sévère	– *strict*
aimable	– *pleasant*	fainéant(e)	– *lazy*
gentil(le)	– *nice, kind*	méchant(e)	– *nasty*
tolérant(e)	– *tolerant*	agressif(ve)	– *aggressive*
patient(e)	– *patient*	injuste	– *unfair*
compréhensif/ve	– *understanding*	effronté(e)	– *cheeky*
doux(ce)	– *gentle*	embêtant(e)	– *annoying*
vif(ve)	– *lively*	étouffant(e)	– *suffocating*
disponible	– *available/there for you*	énervant(e)	– *annoying*

Vocabulary timing game

Look at the adjectives for 2 minutes and then cover over the English side. Time yourself to see how long it takes you to give the correct translation.

If you are feeling confident, repeat the exercise but this time cover the French side.

Be careful with your pronunciation.

How well did you do? Excellent? Bien? Panique? Here is an indication for you.

Translating:

	into English	into French
excellent	30 – 45 seconds	45 seconds – 1 minute
très bien	45 seconds – 1 minute	1 – 1·15 minutes
bien	1 – 1·30 minutes	1·15 – 1·45 minutes
pas mal	1·30 – 1·45 minutes	1·45 – 2·15 minutes
panique (il faut réviser)	1·45 minutes +	2·15 minutes +

TRACK 2

Remember!

If you can pronounce the words correctly they are a lot easier to understand in listening exercises.

Remember!

Adjectives in French agree with the gender of the noun they are describing.

Do not forget to add an 's' in the plural!

This is a fun way to revise vocabulary. So if you did not do too well this time try again and you will see the improvements.

You could also do the same game but write the words down to check your spelling.

Negatives!

We cannot always get on with everyone; therefore you may need to use the negative form with the verb phrases and the adjectives that you have just seen.

As the negative is very important to know and can be used in all the different sections of the Higher programme, now seems the perfect time to revise this point.

- ne ... pas   – *not/don't*
- ne ... rien   – *nothing*
- ne ... jamais   – *never*
- ne ... plus   – *no longer*

- ne ... guère   – *hardly ever*
- ne ... ni ... ni   – *neither ... nor*
- *ne ... personne   – *no one/nobody*
- *ne ... que   – *only*

Please do not panic or turn the page! This will be quick and easy. Promise.

The last four will really impress, so practise using them in your writing. However they are quite difficult to manipulate.

Practise your knowledge of negatives by trying out the multiple-choice quiz that follows.

Remember!

Imagine the negative in French as a sandwich where the auxiliary or main verb is the filling, e.g. ma sœur n'est jamais allée en France – je ne me confie jamais à mon frère.

*ne ... personne, ne ... que do not always follow this rule. Be careful!

TIPS to help improve reading and translating skills

- First read each sentence.
- Decide what the words mean.
- Use a dictionary to look up the words you do not understand.
- Check the grammar and the structure of the sentence.
- Think about translating skills – does your English translation make sense?

Exercise 3 – Test Yourself

1 Which sentence is incorrect?

a   Ma mère n'est pas très abordable.

b   Je ne me pas sens proche de mon frère.

c   Ma sœur n'est pas fainéante.

d   Je ne peux pas faire confiance à ma sœur cadette.

2 Which of the following sentences is correct?

a   Ma sœur ne rien fait à la maison.

b   Mes parents ne mangent rien le matin.

c   Je n'ai senti rien.

d   Il n'a dit rien.

3 Which of the following sentences means 'he no longer speaks to his family'?

   a Il ne parle à personne dans sa famille.

   b Il ne dit rien à sa famille.

   c Il ne parle plus à sa famille.

   d Il ne parle jamais de sa famille.

4 Which two sentences are correct?

   a Je ne me suis jamais confié à ma grand-mère.

   b Il ne fait confiance jamais à sa belle-mère.

   c Ma sœur n'est énervante jamais.

   d Mon ami n'est jamais agressif.

5 Which sentence means 'I trust no one'?

   a Je ne fais personne confiance.

   b Je ne fais pas confiance à personne.

   c Je ne fais pas confiance à quelqu'un.

   d Je ne fais confiance à personne.

6 What is the best translation for the following sentence? 'Je ne me confie qu'aux gens auxquels je fais totalement confiance.'

   a I don't confide in people I don't trust.

   b I only confide myself in people I do totally trust.

   c I don't confide only in people I totally trust.

   d I only confide in people I totally trust.

7 Which of the following sentences means 'I don't feel close to either my older sister or my younger sister'?

   a Je ne me suis proche pas ni de ma sœur aînée ni ma sœur cadette.

   b Je ne fais pas me sentir proche ni de ma sœur aînée ni de ma sœur cadette.

   c Je ne me sens proche ni de ma sœur aînée ni de ma sœur cadette.

   d Je ne me sens pas ni proche de ma sœur aînée ni de ma sœur cadette.

8 Which of the following sentences is incorrect?

   a Ma sœur n'est pas méchante.

   b Mon frère ne se confie plus à moi.

   c Mes parents ne sont pas sévères.

   d Mes amis ne me font confiance plus.

 **Bravo! Tu as réussi!**

Check your answers to see how well you did.

The correct answers have been given to all the incorrect sentences used in this quiz.

All these correct sentences can be used for both speaking and writing practice. Select the sentences that you felt most confident with and try to use them for these purposes.

TOPIC 2 · Family Conflicts – Les Conflits Familiaux

Now as we all know, there can sometimes be disagreements with family and friends.

Try to think of some reasons as to the cause of these conflicts.

Here are some ideas: add some of your own in the other circles.

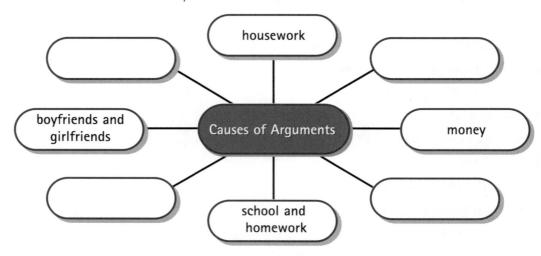

General vocabulary

Here is a list of some vocabulary and expressions that you should be able to use to talk about family conflicts.

• les conflits	– *conflicts*
• les disputes	– *arguments*
• les frictions	– *frictions*
• les bagarres	– *fights/arguments*

Here are some more popular expressions which you can practise on the CD. Use your dictionary to look up the meanings of any words.

TRACK 3

avoir des disputes/des confrontations – *to have arguments*
    exemple, Il y a souvent des disputes à propos des travaux ménagers.
            Il y a souvent des confrontations à cause de l'argent.

se disputer – *to argue*
    exemple, Mes parents et moi nous disputons souvent à propos de mon petit ami/de ma petite amie.

se faire gronder par – *to be told off by*
    exemple, Je me fais toujours gronder par ma mère si je ne fais pas mes devoirs.

reprocher – *to criticise/to reproach*
    exemple, Mes parents me reprochent d'être trop effronté.

créer des tensions – *to create tensions*
    exemple, Il y a souvent des choses qui créent des tensions dans la famille.

ce qui m'énerve – *the thing that annoys me*
    exemple, Ce qui m'énerve chez mes parents c'est qu'ils veulent tout savoir sur ma vie privée.

avoir besoin de demander la permission – *need to ask permission*
    exemple, J'ai toujours besoin de demander la permission si je veux sortir avec mes amis.

Remember!
When looking up verbs you must look up the infinitive to find the meaning, e.g. – 'veulent' is the 'ils' form – you will need to look up 'vouloir' to find the meaning.

Exercise 4 – Practise your translation skills by translating the above sentences into English. Once again all of these sentences can be used in both speaking and writing exercises. It's up to you to select and practise the ones you prefer.

TIPS to improve reading, dictionary, listening and pronunciation skills

- First read each paragraph to get a general understanding.
- Use your dictionary to look up any problem words.
- Before you listen, try to complete the gaps choosing one of the pairs of words in the boxes below. Pay particular attention to spelling and grammar.
- Listen to the CD to check your answers and to fill in the remaining gaps.
- Check your answers and correct the problems – make a list of these problem words.
- Listen again reading the passage at the same time as the speaker on the CD. This will help with your pronunciation of the more difficult words.

Exercise 5 – On the CD you will hear three extracts about disagreements and conflicts within the family.

A De temps en temps il y a de petites .... chez nous. Par ...., moi, je n'aime pas faire les travaux .... comme faire la .... ou passer l'aspirateur. Je ne range jamais ma .... et par conséquent elle est toujours en désordre. Ma mère me .... assez souvent à ce propos. En plus je n'aime ni les .... de télévision que mes parents .... ni la même nourriture et ceci peut créer énormément de tensions entre nous.

TRACK 4

> ménagers/ménagère   chambre/chamber
> émissions/émission   regardent/regarde
> exemple/example   gronde/grondent
> vaisselle/vesselle   disputes/disput

B Je ne m' .... pas toujours très bien avec mes parents car j'estime qu'ils .... trop sévères avec moi. On a souvent des confrontations à propos de mes sorties et de mes .... Cependant, ce qui m'énerve le plus chez eux c'est qu'ils .... mes amis et m'empêchent souvent d'aller en .... avec eux. J'ai .... ans mais ils s'obstinent quand même à me traiter comme un .... et s'occupent trop de ma vie ...., ce qui est trop injuste.

> critiquent/criticent   boîte/boitte
> dix-set/dix-sept   sont/son
> entends/entend   amis/ami
> privé/privée   enfant/infant

C En général je m'entends très bien avec mes parents mais parfois on se .... à propos de mon .... et de l'argent. Tous les .... je travaille dans un .... de vêtements pour gagner un peu d' ...., mais mes parents .... que je devrais passer mes week-ends à .... pour l'école. Je suis très .... aussi, ce qui les énerve d'autant plus.

> trouvent/trouve   dispute/disputent
> argent/arjen   dépensier/dépense
> étudier/étudiaient   éducation/educasion
> magasin/magazin   week-ends/weekends

Once again, the three extracts above can be used for both speaking and writing practice.

You will see from the three extracts that there are many different ways to talk about disagreements within the family. Try to write a passage about conflicts within your family. Use the expressions you have already seen to help you.

Household tasks – les tâches ménagères

Who does or doesn't do their share of household tasks can often cause friction!

When looking at family disagreements we come across household tasks. These always come up in exams and it is extremely important for you to know them. You will already know many of these, but to impress the markers you should try to use some of the more difficult ones. They have been marked with an * asterisk here.

Exercise 6 – Match each picture with the correct phrase from the box below.

> *faire le jardinage   faire son lit   faire le ménage
> *faire la lessive   *faire le repassage   *sortir la poubelle
> passer l'aspirateur   faire la cuisine   *mettre la table

Daily routines – les routines quotidiennes

You will find that the theme of Lifestyles will involve you in revising, consolidating and expanding topics that you studied for Standard Grade. You may want to revise and expand your daily routine when talking about family conflict, as getting up late, going to bed late and staying in the shower too long often cause conflict in the family home.

This is also something that often crops up in listening and reading exercises.

Using the pictures on the next page to help you, write a story about Stéphanie's typical day.

Remember to link your sentences using the following words:

- parce que   – *because*
- car   – *because*
- cependant   – *however*
- néanmoins   – *nevertheless*
- mais   – *but*
- puis/ensuite   – *then/next*

Remember!
Revise frequency adverbs, time phrases and the time, i.e.
– toujours, souvent, de temps en temps, quelquefois, rarement, jamais, etc.
– tous les jours, le matin, le soir, après, avant, etc.
– à une heure, à sept heures et demie, à midi, etc.

- puisque/comme   – *as*
- pour + infinitive   – *in order to*
- afin de + infinitive   – *in order to*
- tandis que   – *at the same time/while*

If you're feeling confident, write the same story but in the past tense. You could use the following:

- ayant + past participle, e.g. ayant mangé   – *having eaten*
- étant + past participle, e.g. étant sorti(e) – *having gone out*
- être with reflexives, e.g. m'étant levé(e)   – *having got up*

You may also wish to write the story using other tenses, i.e. the future, the perfect, etc.

If you need to, use the vocabulary at the bottom of the page to help you.

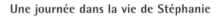

Une journée dans la vie de Stéphanie

Tous les jours Stéphanie ...

 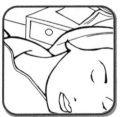

Vocabulaire

- se lever   – *to get up*
- se doucher   – *to have a shower*
- se maquiller   – *to put on make up*
- se coiffer   – *to do one's hair*
- se coucher   – *to go to bed*
- dîner   – *to have dinner*
- faire ses devoirs   – *to do one's homework*
- prendre le petit déjeuner   – *to have breakfast*
- bavarder au téléphone avec ses amis   – *to chat to friends on the phone*
- aller à l'ecole   – *to go to school*

Now write about your typical day.

TOPIC 3 Ideal Parents – Les Parents Idéaux

We have now looked at relationships with families and friends and conflicts within a family. The next theme is 'Ideal Parents – Les Parents Idéaux'.

What in your opinion are the qualities that make good or bad parents?

Exercise 7a – Look at the following list. Rewrite them under the two headings 'good parents' and 'bad parents'.

- Ils s'occupent de leurs enfants.

- Ils sont toujours en train de râler.

- Ils s'intéressent à l'éducation de leurs enfants.

- Ils partent souvent en vacances sans leurs enfants.

- Ils sont très sévères.

- Ils laissent leurs enfants tout faire.

- Ils donnent de bons conseils à leurs enfants.

- Ils traitent tous leurs enfants de la même façon.

- Ils battent leurs enfants.

- Ils sont très compréhensifs et parlent de tout avec leurs enfants.

- Ils font des excursions ensemble.

- Ils gâtent leurs enfants.

- Ils apprennent les bonnes manières, la politesse et le respect des valeurs morales aux enfants.

Now listen to track 5 on the CD to see if you have got the same answers and at the same time practise your pronunciation.

Exercise 7b – If you want to practise your translation skills, try translating all the above sentences into English. Remember to make sure that your English makes sense.

Once again all these expressions can be used for both speaking and writing practice, so select the ones you wish to use.

Exercise 8 – Listen to track 6 on the CD on which three people give their opinion of what makes a good parent.

Take notes on what each person says.

Stéphanie ...

Christophe ...

Thomas ...

TIPS to improve pronunciation and listening skills

- Check your answers.
- Listen again, reading the transcript at the same time, to check any problems you had.
- Practise the pronunciation of the words you had difficulty in hearing the first time.
- Make a list of these words so you can revise them regularly.

Do you agree or disagree with any of the opinions given?

Remember!

Look up the infinitive of verbs, e.g. apprennent – apprendre.

Adjectives will not necessarily have the agreement endings in the dictionary. So you will need to look up the masculine form of the adjective, e.g. compréhensifs – you look up compréhensif.

TRACKS 5 & 6

Remember!

You can use all these expressions in the negative form as well. So remember to revise those negatives again!

Remember!

Correct pronunciation will help improve your understanding of words.

Grammar point!

You will maybe have noticed the frequent use of 'devoir' in the last two passages. As you know this word means 'should, ought, must, have to' and is often used when giving opinions especially when talking hypothetically.

This is one of the modal verbs that you will already have come across at Higher, but it does need to be revised again so that you are able to use it with ease and fluency. Like the other modal verbs (pouvoir/vouloir/savoir/falloir) it is usually followed by the infinitive of a second verb, e.g. il faut partir; ils veulent rentrer.

Devoir: have to, should, ought

Present		Conditional	
je dois	nous devons	je devrais	nous devrions
tu dois	vous devez	tu devrais	vous devriez
il doit	ils doivent	il devrait	ils devraient

Write a passage on what makes good parents in your opinion. Try to justify your opinions.

On the CD you will hear some ways of expressing your opinion on this subject:

A mon avis pour être bon parent, on doit + infinitive ...

Selon moi, les parents idéaux devraient + infinitive ...

Je trouve que de bons parents devraient + infinitive ...

A mon avis un bon parent est quelqu'un qui + verb ...

Selon moi, les parents idéaux sont + adjective ...

TRACK 7

Now you will hear some expressions to help you justify your answer:

... parce que ça apprend aux enfants à être plus polis

... car ça aide les enfants à mieux travailler à l'école

... ça rend les enfants plus indépendants et les prépare pour l'avenir

... ça apprend aux enfants à mieux communiquer avec d'autres personnes.

TRACK 8

A toi maintenant!

Bonne chance!

TOPIC 4 Holidays with or without Parents? – Les Vacances avec ou sans Parents?

Although this topic comes up in the theme The Wider World, now seems like the perfect time to look at this topic as many of the expressions you have already seen can and should be used when talking about holidays with your parents.

We will therefore begin by looking at the advantages and disadvantages of going on holiday with your parents.

Here are some ideas, but feel free to add any extra expressions that you can think of. They have been included on the CD to help with your pronunciation.

TRACK 9

Les avantages	Les inconvénients
Ils nous payent tout ce que nous voulons.	Ils ne s'amusent pas de la même façon.
On se sent plus en sécurité.	Ils ne nous laissent rien faire tous seuls.
On peut faire des excursions ensemble.	Il faut tout le temps aller avec eux.
Ils nous amènent au restaurant.	On n'aime pas les mêmes choses.
Ils s'occupent de nous.	Il faut toujours demander la permission si on veut sortir en boîte.
Ils portent les valises.	On se dispute plus souvent.
Ils s'occupent de tous les papiers.	Ils peuvent être humiliants.

Dictionary work

Use your dictionary to check any words you do not understand.

Exercise 9 – Try translating the above sentences into English to help you with your translation skills.

If you were preparing a talk or writing a short essay on this topic, you may wish to begin by using one of the following:

TRACK 10

- <u>Je vais vous parler des avantages et des inconvénients de</u> partir en vacances avec ses parents.

- <u>Je vais vous parler des avantages et des inconvénients qu'il y a</u> à partir en vacances en famille.

- <u>Je vais vous expliquer pourquoi je préfère</u> partir en vacances avec mes parents au lieu de mes amis.

- Je pars toujours en vacances avec mes parents et <u>je vais vous expliquer les avantages de</u> ce genre de voyage.

- <u>Selon moi, il y a beaucoup d'avantages et d'inconvénients de</u> partir en vacances en famille/avec ses parents.

The words underlined can be used as an introduction to any topic.

Select the ones you prefer and try to use them when preparing a talk or a piece of writing.

These sentences are on the CD to help your pronunciation.

> **Remember!**
> Look up the infinitives of verbs, e.g. s'occupent (is the 'ils' form) so look up s'occuper in the dictionary to find the correct meaning.

Still within the theme The Wider World, we look at ideal holidays.

What would be your ideal holiday?

This could be one of the essay topics, so let's brainstorm some ideas.

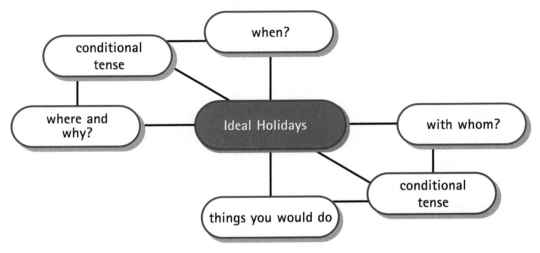

As you can see from the above diagram all the bubbles are connected to the 'conditional tense'.

As you are talking about an ideal holiday, you will need to use the conditional tense, which is translated by 'would' in English.

Yes, it's grammar time again. A quick revision of the conditional. Really easy this one.

Conditional tense

Regular verbs – take the infinitive of any verb and add the 'imperfect' endings.

e.g. – aimer

j'aimer**ais**	nous aimer**ions**
tu aimer**ais**	vous aimer**iez**
il/elle aimer**ait**	ils/elles aimer**aient**

There are of course exceptions which must be learned. These include (with the 'il' form):

avoir – aurait, aller – irait, être – serait, devoir – devrait, savoir – saurait, falloir – faudrait, etc.

Dictionary skills

Read each sentence first to get a general idea.

Decide on the important words and look these up in the dictionary if you don't understand them.

Most of the verbs below are in the conditional tense and once again you will need to look up the infinitive of these verbs for the meaning,

e.g.   aimerais – look up aimer

         irais is irregular and the infinitive is 'aller'.

There will be a section on irregular verbs in your dictionary. This will be either at the back of your dictionary or in the middle.

Exercise 10 – Practise your translation skills by translating the following sentences into English.

Where would I spend my ideal holiday and why? – Où passerais-je mes vacances idéales et pourquoi?

J'irais dans un pays chaud en hiver pour éviter la pluie et le froid de Glasgow.

J'aimerais faire le tour du monde pour visiter tous les pays qui m'intéressent.

Mon rêve est d'aller au Japon afin d'y découvrir la culture japonaise.

J'aimerais aller sur une île déserte pour me détendre et profiter de sa tranquillité.

J'aimerais bien aller à New York pour visiter tous les monuments, me promener dans 'Central Park' et faire du shopping dans tous les magasins de luxe.

It's your turn – Où aimerais-tu aller en vacances et pourquoi?

When? – Quand?

Les saisons – en hiver, en été, en automne, au printemps

Les mois – j'irais au mois de janvier/février, etc.

Age – quand je serai plus vieux/vieille

It's your turn – Quand aimerais-tu y aller?

With whom? – Avec qui?

J'irais avec ma meilleure amie/mon meilleur ami parce qu'on s'amuserait bien ensemble.

Je crois que j'irais en famille car je pourrais profiter de la générosité de mes parents et bien sûr on passerait de très bonnes vacances ensemble.

J'irais en vacances tout(e) seul(e) car c'est la meilleure façon de rencontrer d'autres gens et de faire ce que l'on veut.

It's your turn – Avec qui irais-tu?

Things you would do? – Que ferais-tu?

There are obviously many possibilities but here are a few. Feel free to add your own ideas.

J'irais souvent au restaurant pour y déguster les spécialités du pays.

Je visiterais beaucoup de monuments célèbres, de galeries d'art, etc.

Je passerais mes journées sur la plage avec un bon roman.

Je ferais beaucoup de sport comme du ski, du patinage et des randonnées.

J'essayerais de parler avec les gens de là-bas pour mieux connaître leur culture et améliorer mon français/espagnol/allemand, etc.

It's your turn – Que ferais-tu?

All of the above sentences and phrases can be used for both speaking and writing practice.

Select the ones you prefer and try to use them when preparing your talk or piece of writing on this topic.

Exercise 11 – On the CD you will hear four people talking about their ideal holiday.

For each person, give an answer as to **where** and **why**, **when**, **with whom** and **what they would do there**.

Now check your answers.

TRACK 11   Look at the transcript to see where you had problems.

Listen to the CD again, reading the transcript at the same time.

This will help you with your pronunciation of any difficult words.

Test yourself

Exercise 12 – What do the following words mean?

- avoir de bon rapport avec quelqu'un

- bien s'entendre avec quelqu'un

- méchant

- avoir une sœur cadette

- donner de bons conseils

- découvrir

- faire le repassage

- tandis que

- afin de

Remember!
You can use all of the vocabulary and sentences in these listening extracts to help you prepare for a talk or a piece of writing on this topic.

Exercise 13 – Complete the sentences using the correct form of the adjectives given:

Mes parents sont très …	(available/there for you)
Ma sœur est toujours très …	(annoying)
Mes frères sont …	(lazy)
Ma grand-mère est … mais …	(old, lively)
Mon père est …	(funny)
Mon frère est quelquefois …	(aggressive)
Ma mère est …	(tolerant)
Mes sœurs sont …	(understanding)

Exercise 14 – Translate the following sentences:

Je me dispute souvent avec ma sœur cadette.

Les parents ne devraient pas gâter leurs enfants.

Après avoir pris mon petit déjeuner, je me suis brossé les dents.

J'irais en vacances avec mes parents car on s'entend très bien ensemble.

J'aimerais aller dans un pays chaud en hiver pour éviter le froid et la pluie de l'Ecosse.

TOPIC 6 Home Area – Chez Soi

Let's brainstorm some ideas.

Add any other ideas you may have.

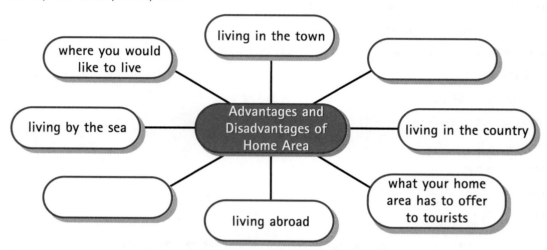

As you can see from the diagram, you will be required to give advantages and disadvantages of living in different areas and where you would prefer to live. The conditional tense and negatives will again be used here, so revise these again!

Here is a list of general vocabulary that you may wish to use during this section.

Try the 'vocabulary timing game' to see how long it takes you to learn them.

Bonne chance!

General vocabulary

- habiter en ville — to live in town
- vivre à la campagne — to live in the country
- bien s'amuser — to have a good time/to enjoy oneself
- éviter le stress — to avoid stress
- avoir peur — to be afraid

- la vie nocturne — nightlife
- le bruit — noise
- les pots d'échappements — exhaust pipes
- une ville industrielle — an industrial town
- les centres commerciaux — shopping centres
- reposant — relaxing
- les espaces verts — green areas
- le paysage — the scenery
- les attractions touristiques — sights

- trop de — too much/many
- beaucoup de — a lot of
- assez de — enough of
- peu de — few/not much/not many

How did you do?

Keep practising and use the vocabulary regularly as it will help you to remember it.

Now for some listening!

On the CD you will hear ten sentences for each area you can live in, i.e. in the town, in the country or by the sea.

Specific vocabulary for listening exercise

- les divertissements — *entertainment*
- l'anonymat — *anonymity*
- les transports en commun — *public transport*
- un appartement convenable — *suitable apartment*
- les loyers — *the rent*
- aux alentours — *round about/in the vicinity*
- être au courant — *to know about something*
- s'ennuyer — *to get bored*
- gênant — *annoying, embarrassing*
- se détendre — *to relax*
- s'inquiéter — *to worry*
- la saleté — *the dirt*
- la rouille — *rust*
- les encombrements — *congestion*

- Before listening read each sentence.
- Use your dictionary to check the meanings of the words you do not understand.
- Practise your translation skills by translating the sentences into English.

Remember!

Remember all of the sentences can be used when preparing a talk or a piece of writing. Choose the ones you feel most comfortable with.

Exercise 15 – Now listen to each sentence remembering to practise the pronunciation.

Number each one as you hear it and then rewrite the sentences under the headings – **positive aspects** or **negative aspects**.

Habiter en ville – living in town

Il y a beaucoup de voitures et par conséquent trop de pollution.

Il y a beaucoup de choses à faire et à voir.

On peut se sentir seul car il y a un fort anonymat en ville.

Il y a énormément de divertissements à proximité.

On n'est pas obligé d'avoir une voiture car il y a de bons transports en commun.

La vie en ville peut être stressante à cause du bruit et de la circulation.

Il y a trop de monde en ville et par conséquent on est toujours stressé.

Il n'y a pas assez d'espaces verts.

Il y a beaucoup de crime en ville et donc on ne se sent pas toujours en sécurité.

Les loyers en ville sont très élevés et c'est donc très difficile de trouver un appartement convenable.

TRACK 12

TRACK 13

Vivre à la campagne – living in the country

On peut profiter de la nature et de la tranquillité.

Il n'y a pas beaucoup de circulation et par conséquent peu de bruit et de pollution.

Il n'y a rien aux alentours et on s'ennuie facilement.

Tout le monde connaît ses voisins alors on ne se sent jamais seul.

Tout le monde est toujours au courant de tout ce qu'on fait ce qui peut parfois être gênant.

Il y a peu de possibilités de travail, alors beaucoup de jeunes quittent la campagne pour aller chercher du travail en ville.

La campagne n'est pas bien desservie par les transports en commun et il faut donc souvent avoir une voiture pour se déplacer.

Les gens sont moins stressés à la campagne et on arrive à mieux se détendre.

L'air est pur et on peut se promener tranquillement dans les champs sans se sentir étouffé par le bruit et la saleté en ville.

C'est très agréable pour les enfants parce que les parents peuvent les laisser jouer dehors sans s'inquiéter.

TRACK 14

Vivre au bord de la mer – living by the sea

Le paysage est vraiment beau malgré le temps.

On se sent toujours en vacances parce que la plage est à proximité.

Les odeurs de poisson et de la mer peuvent parfois être désagréables.

En été il y a beaucoup de touristes et les résidents de la ville se plaignent des encombrements qu'ils provoquent.

Il y a toujours beaucoup de travail en été pour les étudiants.

En hiver la mer est souvent très agitée et ça peut être très dangereux.

Lorsqu'il fait beau on peut passer ses journées à la plage sans dépenser d'argent.

On peut faire beaucoup de sports aquatiques ce qui est vraiment super.

Le bruit de la mer est très paisible et aide à se détendre.

Il y a souvent du brouillard ce qui peut être très dangereux pour conduire.

Les voitures sont vite rouillées à cause de l'air marin.

Now it's your turn

Below are eight sentences for you to complete which will help you when writing about this subject.

Complete the sentences using the phrases you have just seen or heard.

A mon avis la vie en ville est agréable parce que ...

J'adore vivre en ville car ...

Selon moi, la vie en ville n'est pas très agréable car ...

Les inconvénients de vivre en ville sont que ...

Il y a beaucoup d'avantages et d'inconvénients à vivre à la campagne. Les avantages sont que ...

Je trouve que vivre à la campagne est mieux que de vivre en ville parce que …

Je n'aime pas vivre à la campagne parce que …

Les raisons pour lesquelles j'adore vivre au bord de la mer sont que …

The above sentences have been included on the CD to help your pronunciation.

TRACK 15

You may wish to use some sentences to say where you would or wouldn't want to live. As previously said, you will have to use the conditional tense here.

Here are a few examples of how you could start the sentences. Remember the place can change and any of the sentences that you have already seen and heard in this section could be used to complete the following phrases.

However, please ensure that it makes sense.

- Use a dictionary to look up any words you do not understand.
- Look up the infinitive of verbs and be careful with the future and conditional tenses
- Remember   'quitterai' = will leave

                            'aimerais' = would like

Where you would like to live

J'aimerais mieux vivre en ville/à la campagne/au bord de la mer parce que …

Quand je quitterai l'école, je voudrais vivre en ville, parce que …

J'ai toujours rêvé de vivre au bord de la mer, parce que …

Quand je serai plus vieux (vieille) j'aimerais vivre en ville, car …

Where you wouldn't like to live

Je ne pourrais jamais vivre en ville, car …

Je ne quitterais jamais la ville pour vivre à la campagne parce que …

Je ne serais pas heureux(se) si je vivais à la campagne car …

Je n'aimerais pas habiter en ville, parce que …

TRACK 16

TRACK 17

Practise writing some sentences using these phrases. You may also wish to say that you would like to live abroad. Although you will come across reasons for this in the **'Education and Work'** section and the **'Directed Writing'** section, here are just a few examples of what you could use.

J'aimerais vivre à l'étranger parce que j'adore découvrir d'autres cultures et rencontrer les gens de pays différents.

Quand j'aurai fini mes études, j'aimerais vivre en France car j'adore la culture et la cuisine française et je pourrais y améliorer mon français.

J'ai toujours rêvé de vivre en France car c'est un très beau pays où il y a beaucoup de choses intéressantes à voir et à découvrir.

Test yourself

Exercise 16 – What do the following words mean?

- les divertissements
- s'inquiéter
- s'ennuyer
- les transports en commun
- les loyers
- aux alentours
- gênant
- se détendre
- la rouille

Exercise 17 – Translate the following sentences into English:

1 J'aime vivre en ville parce que c'est plus animé que la campagne.

2 La vie à la campagne est tranquille et reposante.

3 Il y a trop de pollution en ville à cause des nombreux véhicules.

4 Je n'aimerais pas vivre à la campagne car c'est trop isolé.

5 Je ne voudrais pas vivre au bord de la mer car j'ai peur de l'eau.

6 La vie à la campagne est trop ennuyeuse.

7 Il y a beaucoup de crime en ville et par conséquent c'est très dangereux.

Exercise 18 – Correct the word(s) underlined (you may have to add or remove some words):

Il y a beaucoup <u>de la</u> circulation en ville.

Il n'y a pas assez <u>des</u> divertissements à la campagne.

Il y a un grand nombre <u>des</u> restaurants en ville.

Il y a peu <u>des</u> choses <u>intéressant</u> à faire à la campagne.

La vie est <u>cherer</u> en ville qu'à la campagne.

Healthy living is one of the big topics in the Higher programme, so let's brainstorm the different areas that we will need to cover in this section.

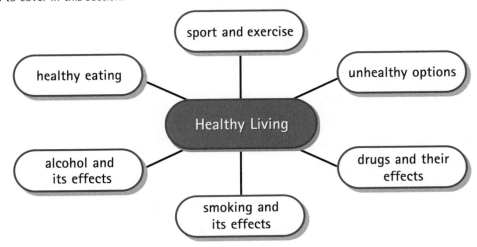

Sport and Healthy Diet

Grammar point!

During this section you will come across 'modal' verbs again. We have already looked at 'devoir' and this should be revised again.

Here is some general vocabulary that you will be using throughout this first section. Try the 'vocabulary timing game' to see how long it takes you to learn it.

General vocabulary

- être en bonne santé — *to be in good health*
- être en pleine forme — *to be on form*
- se tenir en pleine forme — *to stay in good form*
- rester en bonne santé — *to stay in good health*
- manger équilibré — *to eat a balanced diet*
- une alimentation équilibrée — *a balanced diet*
- manger une nourriture saine — *to eat healthy food*
- une alimentation saine — *a healthy diet*
- une vie saine — *a healthy lifestyle*
- de la nourriture grasse — *fatty food*
- grignoter entre les repas — *to eat between meals*
- sauter les repas — *to skip meals*
- surveiller son alimentation — *to watch one's diet*
- garder la ligne — *to keep your figure*
- les courbatures — *aches/stiffness*
- être nuisible — *to be harmful*
- digérer — *to digest*
- faire du sport — *to do sport*
- faire de l'exercice — *to do sport*
- pratiquer un sport — *to do a sport*
- prendre du poids — *to gain weight*
- perdre du poids — *to lose weight*
- faire un régime — *to go on a diet*

Remember!

You will also be using 'il faut/il ne faut pas' + infinitive meaning 'it is necessary to/you have to'.

Remember!

A lot of sports take 'faire' in French – revise these.

TRACK 18

The following phrases are examples of how you could start talking about healthy lifestyles.

Exercise 19a – Listen to the CD and complete the sentences by writing what the people say.

Check your answers.

Make a list of any problem words you encountered.

Listen again to practise the pronunciation.

Exercise 19b – Try translating each sentence into English.

1   Pour être en bonne santé, il faut ...

2   Pour se maintenir en forme, on doit ...

3   Pour garder la ligne, il faut ...

4   Ce qui est bon pour la santé, c'est de ...

5   A mon avis le secret d'une bonne santé, c'est de ...

You may also want to say what is bad for your health and the effects of this.

Exercise 20a – Complete these sentences by choosing from the appropriate phrases.

Il ne faut pas grignoter entre les repas parce que ...

On ne devrait pas boire trop de boissons sucrées car ...

Il ne faut pas trop manger le soir parce que ...

Une nourriture trop grasse ...

Il ne faut pas sauter les repas car ...

Il ne faut pas beaucoup manger avant de faire du sport car ...

Si on ne fait pas de sport ...

Il faut toujours s'échauffer avant de faire du sport pour ...

Phrases to complete the sentences:

... est nuisible à la santé et peut provoquer des problèmes de cholestérol

... ça fait grossir

... ne pas se déchirer les muscles et pour éviter les courbatures

... on a besoin de la nourriture pour apporter de l'énergie à notre corps

... le sucre est très mauvais pour les dents et peut créer des caries

... on devient fainéant et le corps se rouille

... ça nous empêche de bien dormir

... la nourriture a besoin d'être bien digérée pour éviter les crampes.

Exercise 20b – Try translating these sentences into English.

TIPS to help improve reading and translating skills

- Read the sentences to get a general idea.
- Think of possible ways of completing the sentences before looking at the phrases.
- Now look at the phrases. Try to complete the sentences.
- Use your dictionary to look up any words you do not understand and make a list of these.
- Practise your translation skills by translating the sentences into English.

Smoking/Drugs/Alcohol – La Cigarette/La Drogue/L'Alcool

Here is a list of some vocabulary that may be useful for this section.

Try the 'vocabulary timing game' to help you remember the vocabulary.

General vocabulary

- substances nocives   – *harmful substances*
- se droguer   – *to take drugs*
- prendre de la drogue   – *to take drugs*
- fumer   – *to smoke*
- boire trop d'alcool   – *to drink too much alcohol*
- néfaste   – *harmful*
- les poumons   – *lungs*
- le foie   – *liver*
- les maladies cardio-vasculaires – *heart diseases*
- grave   – *serious*
- le système sanguin   – *blood circulation*
- avoir mauvaise haleine   – *to have bad breath*
- la peau   – *the skin*
- le cerveau   – *the brain*
- dangereux   – *dangerous*

Smoking, drugs and alcohol are a major threat to our health, so why do so many people abuse these substances?

Pourquoi commence-t-on à fumer/boire/prendre de la drogue?

- Before listening to the CD, read the phrases below.
- Read them aloud to practise your pronunciation.
- Use your dictionary to help you with any words you do not understand and to check on the correct meaning.

Exercise 21a – Now listen to the CD and put the following sentences in order as you hear them. Check your pronunciation of the sentences by reading the sentences at the same time.

TRACK 19

Les gens fument/boivent trop d'alcool/prennent de la drogue ...
- pour faire comme les autres/les amis/les parents
- par souci d'appartenance à un groupe social
- parce qu'ils sont influencés par les amis
- pour avoir l'air cool
- pour perdre du poids
- pour le plaisir
- pour oublier les problèmes familiaux
- à cause du stress de la société
- pour échapper à la réalité.

Exercise 21b – You can also practise your translation skills by translating the above sentences into English.

Remember that these sentences can be used when preparing a talk or a piece of writing.

Choose the ones you wish to use.

The Effects of Smoking – Les Effets de la Cigarette

Read the following sentences, then listen to them on the CD. Remember to use a dictionary if needed.

TRACK 20

La nicotine est très néfaste pour notre système sanguin.

Elle nuit au corps et à la santé.

La fumée est nocive pour le fumeur ainsi que le non-fumeur.

La fumée pique les yeux et pollue l'air ambiant.

La cigarette donne mauvaise haleine et jaunit les dents.

Les fumeurs ont souvent les doigts jaunes.

La cigarette est responsable de grave maladies comme:

– l'asthme

– les troubles cardiaques

– le cancer.

La cigarette rend la peau grise et la fait vieillir prématurément.

Specific vocabulary

• jaunir les dents   – *to make your teeth yellow*

Remember all the sentences here can be used when preparing a talk or a piece of writing.

Exercise 22 – Practise your translation skills by translating them into English.

The Effects of Alcohol – Les Effets de l'Alcool

Read the following sentences, then listen to them on the CD. Remember to use a dictionary if needed.

L'alcool n'a pas une grande valeur nutritionnelle et peut faire grossir.

L'alcool donne mauvaise haleine.

Consommer de l'alcool de manière irresponsable peut être dangereux pour soi ainsi que pour ses proches.

TRACK 21

Trop d'alcool peut provoquer de graves maladies comme:

– les maladies cardio-vasculaires

– le cancer du foie.

L'alcool affecte le cerveau et affaiblit nos facultés physiques et mentales.

On ne sait plus ce qu'on fait lorsqu'on boit trop d'alcool.

Trop d'alcool rend souvent les gens violents.

Specific vocabulary
- dangereux pour soi
- affaiblit nos facultés

   – *dangerous for oneself*
   – *weakens our faculties*

Remember all the sentences here can be used when preparing a talk or a piece of writing.

Exercise 23 – Practise your translation skills by translating them into English.

The Effects of Drug Use – Les Effets de la Drogue

Read the following sentences, then listen to them on the CD. Remember to use a dictionary if needed.

TRACK 22

La drogue affecte les réflexes.

Elle est très dangereuse pour le cerveau et le système sanguin.

La prise de drogue peut engendrer de graves maladies.

La drogue peut coûter cher.

La drogue et la criminalité sont souvent liées.

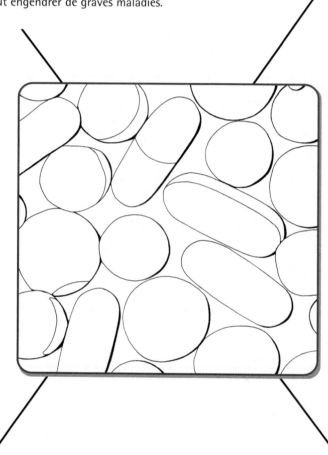

La drogue affecte le comportement social.

La vie normale s'écroule.

Ça mène parfois à la solitude.

Certaines drogues conduisent à la dépendance.

La drogue peut faire de l'homme une épave.

A un certain stade il devient difficile de s'en passer.

Specific vocabulary:

- être lié à   – to go together/to be connected to
- s'écrouler   – to collapse
- une épave   – a wreck
- se passer de   – to do without

Remember all the sentences here can be used when preparing a talk or a piece of writing.

Exercise 24 – Practise your translation skills by translating them into English.

The Solutions – Les Solutions

Look at the following sentences which suggest solutions to the problems of drugs, cigarettes and alcohol.

- Use your dictionary to look up any words you do not understand.
- Remember 'il faut' means: we must/we have to.
- Exercise 25 – Practise your translation skills by translating the sentences into English.
- Add any more ideas that you may have.

Pour décourager/dissuader les jeunes de prendre ces substances abusives ...

Il faut augmenter les campagnes publicitaires exposant les dangers de la drogue/de la cigarette/de l'alcool.

Il faut encourager les parents et l'école à leur parler de ses dangers aussitôt que possible.

On doit en parler ouvertement et insister sur les effets néfastes de la drogue/de la cigarette/de l'alcool.

On doit interdire les affiches publicitaires.

These sentences have been included on the CD to help your pronunciation.

TRACK 23

Focus on Listening/Writing

Listening can often be difficult, so here is a strategy you can use to help you improve your listening skills.

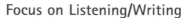

TIPS to help improve listening skills

Always read ALL the questions before you listen to the recording so you can have a general idea of the vocabulary you need to listen for.

Before listening
- Try to think of the key words in the foreign language that you should be listening out for in each question.

First listening
- Get the overall picture – what is the listening about?
- General ideas + key words

Second listening
- The detail – more precise vocabulary, grammar, negatives, numbers, etc.

Third listening
- Complete any gaps you may still have.

Exercise 26 – On y va – let's start

First
Read ALL the following questions about an interview with Julien. Think about possible answers.
For each question, make a list of key words/vocabulary in French that you think you should be listening out for. Now listen to the interview with Julien and tick off any of the vocabulary you hear.

Secondly
Listen again and try to add more vocabulary to your list.
Try to get more of the detail.
Try to answer some of the questions.

Finally
Listen again and complete any gaps you may have.
Answer the questions in English.

Une interview avec Julien

1 What three things does Julien think are important in order to stay healthy?

2 True or false – Julien eats a lot of fatty food. *Vocabulary/key words: matière grasse, nourriture grasse*

3 What is Julien's weakness when it comes to food? *Vocabulary/key words: faiblesse*

4 True or false – Julien loves sport. How do we know this? (Mention the frequency.)

5 Julien gives a reason as to why he thinks people start taking substances such as drugs, etc. What reason does he give?

6 Julien seems to have first-hand experience of the effects these substances can have on the body. What example does he give? (Mention the age.)

7 Name the three places that Julien thinks should do more to inform young people of the effects of such substances.

8 What does Julien think the effects of a 'healthy diet, some sport and avoidance' of harmful substances would have on our body?

TRACK 24

Now check your answers.

If you find that you have missed out a lot of information, look at the transcript to see where you went wrong.

Listen to the CD again and read the transcript at the same time.

You may find the problem is to do with pronunciation and therefore not recognising rather than not understanding the vocabulary. Practise the pronunciation of any words you had difficulty with and make a list of these words.

Now try to write an essay of your own selecting from the vocabulary and expressions you have seen and heard in this unit.

You have been given some guidelines and sentences to help you (which have been included on the CD). However, if you prefer to use your own version, you can do so.

- Remember to use a dictionary to look up any words you do not understand.

- Do not, however, take the first meaning you see as this may not be the correct one.

- Always check all the meanings of the words and choose the one that best fits the context of your sentence.

Part one – the introduction and outline

e.g. – to help you

TRACK 25

- Je vais vous donner mes opinions sur la façon de rester en bonne santé. D'abord je parlerai de ce qu'il faut manger et faire pour se tenir en forme. Ensuite je vous donnerai mes avis sur les substances nocives comme la drogue et l'alcool.

- Je vais vous expliquer comment, selon moi, on peut se maintenir en forme. Je commencerai par la nourriture et le sport. Puis je donnerai mes avis sur la drogue/l'alcool et la cigarette et leurs effets sur notre corps.

Part two – sport and food

Part three – the things you should not do and their effects

Part four – harmful substances and their effects

Part five – conclusion

e.g. – to help you conclude

TRACK 26

- Pour conclure, je pense que pour se tenir en forme on doit d'abord se sentir bien dans sa peau et éviter toutes les substances qui abusent notre corps.

- Pour finir, je dirais que pour rester en bonne santé il faut avoir une alimentation variée et faire un peu de sport. On doit boire avec modération et ne prendre ni drogue ni cigarette.

Now it's your turn.

Test yourself

Exercise 27 – What do the following words mean?

- une alimentation variée

- une nourriture saine

- être en bonne santé

- une vie saine

- faire un régime

- prendre de la drogue

- néfaste

- les poumons

- les substances nocives

Exercise 28 – Translate the following sentences into English:

1 Un régime équilibré nous permet de rester en bonne santé.

2 Pour se maintenir en pleine forme il faut une alimentation saine et faire du sport.

3 Il ne faut pas sauter les repas si on ne veut pas perdre son énergie physique.

4 De temps en temps, on peut se permettre de manger de la nourriture riche.

5 Il faut faire un peu de sport comme de l'aérobic si on veut garder la ligne.

6 Le sport est un bon moyen de se détendre et de rester en forme.

7 Beaucoup de gens commencent à fumer pour faire comme leurs amis.

8 Certaines personnes fument pour combattre le stress.

9 La cigarette provoque beaucoup de maladies graves.

10 Je n'aimerais pas me sentir dépendant d'une drogue.

11 Il faut boire de l'alcool avec modération. Sinon, ça peut être très dangereux.

12 Notre société doit faire plus pour dissuader les jeunes de prendre de la drogue.

Exercise 29 – Correct the word(s) underlined:

Il faut manger <u>beacoup</u> de légumes et de fruits.

Une nourriture <u>sain</u> est indispensable pour rester en pleine forme.

Je <u>fait</u> beaucoup de sport pour me maintenir en forme.

Il y a un grand nombre <u>des</u> personnes qui <u>fume</u> de plus en plus jeune.

TOPIC 8 Television and Films – La Télévision et Les Films

If you are asked to write about TV, you may wish to include the following:

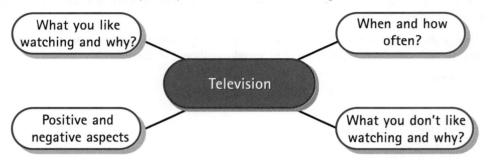

- What you like watching and why?
- When and how often?
- Television
- Positive and negative aspects
- What you don't like watching and why?

General vocabulary

Here is some general vocabulary you will need to remember when talking about television.

- c'est éducatif — *it is educational*
- informer — *to inform*
- divertir — *to entertain*
- enseigner — *to teach*
- instruire — *to instruct/to teach*
- devenir mollasson — *become lazy/lethargic/sluggish*
- devenir pantouflard — *become a person who stays at home all the time*
- abêtir — *to make one stupid*
- amollir — *to weaken/to go soft*
- s'intéresser à — *to be interested in*

Remember!
Revise all the different types of TV programmes.

As television can be considered as a leisure activity, here is a little reminder of some other vocabulary for leisure interests. All the verbs are in the infinitive so ensure you are able to manipulate all the tenses correctly.

Remember to do the 'vocabulary timing game' to help you learn the vocabulary.

Specific vocabulary for leisure activities

- se passionner pour — *to have a passion for something/to be fascinated about something*
- faire de la musique — *to make music*
- écouter de la musique — *to listen to music*
- jouer du piano, etc. — *to play the piano, etc.*
- aller en boîte/au cinéma — *to go to discos/to the cinema*
- faire du sport — *to do sport*
- sortir avec ses amis — *to go out with friends*
- peindre — *to paint*
- faire du bricolage — *to do DIY*
- faire du vélo — *to go cycling*
- cuisiner de bons repas — *to cook good meals*
- marcher/se promener — *to go walking*
- jardiner — *to do gardening*
- pêcher — *to go fishing/to fish*
- la lecture — *reading*

We shall now take each point in turn and develop the ideas.

When and how often – Quand?

Exercise 30 – Translate the following phrases:
tous les jours
les week-ends
jamais
quand il pleut

Exercise 31 – Now listen to the five people on the CD and write down how often they watch TV.

TRACK 27

What you like watching and why? – Que regardes-tu et pourquoi?

Here are some examples. Remember to use your dictionary to look up any words that you do not understand.

Exercise 32 – You can try translating them into English.

• Je préfère regarder les émissions sur la nature et les animaux car je les trouve intéressantes et elles nous apprennent beaucoup de choses.

• J'adore les feuilletons et je ne pourrais jamais les manquer. On veut toujours en connaître la suite.

• Moi, ce que j'aime à la télé, ce sont les films, en particulier les films étrangers et sous-titrés. Ça me permet d'écouter une autre langue et de voir d'autres acteurs peu connus en Grande Bretagne.

TIPS for the gap fill exercises

> • First ensure you understand the general idea using your dictionary if necessary.
> • Try to complete some of the gaps before listening.
> • Listen to the CD to check your answers and add any more.
> • If you have any problems completing the gaps read the transcript and listen to the CD at the same time.
> • Practise the pronunciation of the words to help you remember them.
> • You can also practise your translation skills by translating the examples given.

Exercise 33a – Listen to the three people explaining what they like watching and why and complete the sentences:

1 Je n'aime .... que les .... à la télé car ça me .... d'être au courant des événements ....

2 J'adore les .... parce qu'ils sont très .... et nous aident à sortir de la .... journalière.

3 J'aime beaucoup regarder les .... surtout l'athlétisme. Je fais .... et voir le professionnalisme de ces gens me .... plus.

Exercise 33b – Try translating them into English.

TRACK 28

What you don't like watching and why? – Qu'est-ce que tu n'aimes pas regarder et pourquoi?

Exercise 34 – Try translating the following setences into English. Remember to use your dictionary to look up any difficult words.

• Ce que je ne supporte pas à la télé ce sont les dessins animés. Je les trouve ridicules et ils ne nous apprennent rien d'important.

• J'ai horreur des jeux à la télé. Il y en a beaucoup trop et je trouve que l'argent gagné par les participants pourrait aider des gens qui en ont plus besoin.

• Je ne regarde jamais les films à la télé parce que je préfère les voir au cinéma sur un grand écran. Ça rend le film plus captivant et crée une atmosphère plus réelle.

Exercise 35a – Listen to three people talking and complete the sentences.

1 Je déteste les .... à la télé et je ne les regarde .... Dès qu'on commence à les regarder, on ne peut plus .... C'est vraiment comme une ....

TRACK 29

2 J'ai vraiment du mal à regarder les .... biographiques. Je les trouve peu .... et parfois un peu ....

3 Je déteste les .... car je ne les trouve absolument pas .... De plus, on est forcé d'écouter les .... d'une audience qui n'est même pas .... et honnêtement ça m'énerve ....

Remember to check your answers and pronunciation.

Exercise 35b – Now try translating these sentences into English.

All the sentences and listening extracts that you have just seen and heard can be used when preparing your talk or a piece of writing.

Just be selective about the ones you choose.

Write a passage about:
– how often you watch TV
– what you like and why
– what you don't like and why.

Positive Aspects

You may also be asked to write or speak about the positive aspects of television. Here are some ideas you could include:

A mon avis, il y a plusieurs aspects positifs:

TRACK 30

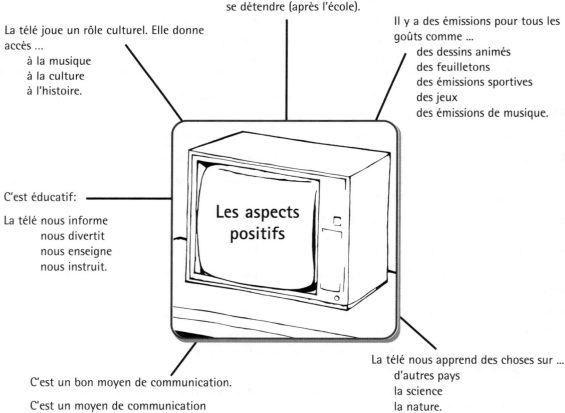

La télé est un bon moyen de ...
découvrir de nouveaux horizons
découvrir d'autres cultures
se détendre (après l'école).

Il y a des émissions pour tous les goûts comme ...
des dessins animés
des feuilletons
des émissions sportives
des jeux
des émissions de musique.

La télé joue un rôle culturel. Elle donne accès ...
à la musique
à la culture
à l'histoire.

C'est éducatif:

La télé nous informe
nous divertit
nous enseigne
nous instruit.

Les aspects positifs

C'est un bon moyen de communication.

C'est un moyen de communication extraordinaire.

La télé nous apprend des choses sur ...
d'autres pays
la science
la nature.

The above sentences have been included on the CD to help your pronunciation.

Exercise 36 – You can also try translating these sentences into English.

Negative Aspects

You may also be asked to write or speak about the negative aspects of television. Here are some ideas you could include which are also on the CD:

Malheureusement il y a plusieurs aspects négatifs comme:

Certaines émissions sont idiotes/banales.

Il y a trop de feuilletons qui sont plus idiots les uns que les autres.

Certaines séries sont interminables.

Il y a trop ...
    de bêtises
    de jeux
    d'émissions idiotes
    d'émissions de qualité médiocre
    de dessins animés.

La télé est surchargée de publicité ridicule et inutile.

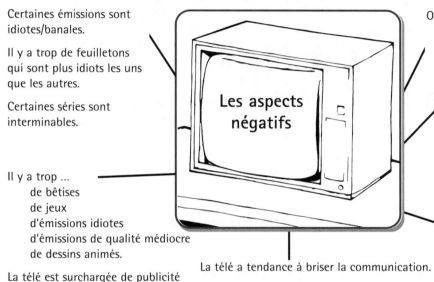

La télé a tendance à briser la communication.

On ne parle plus à autrui.

On court le risque ...
    de devenir mollasson
    de devenir pantouflard.

Il y en a qui ne peuvent pas s'en passer.

Il y a trop de gens qui passent leur vie devant 'le petit écran'.

La télé nous abêtit
    nous ramollit
    nous rend fainéant.

La télé peut empêcher les gens de faire d'autre choses plus intéressantes.

TRACK 31

Exercise 37 – You can try translating these sentences into English.

Vocabulary
- autrui — *others*
- briser — *to break*

Test yourself

Exercise 38 – What do the following words mean?
- les dessins animés
- de temps en temps
- les informations
- le grand écran
- briser la communication
- les feuilletons
- les jeux
- jardiner
- éducatif
- se passionner pour

Exercise 39 – Translate the following sentences into English:

A mon avis, la télé est un moyen de communication extraordinaire.

La télévision nous apprend beaucoup sur d'autres pays et d'autres cultures.

La télé m'aide à me détendre après une longue journée à l'école.

Selon moi, la télévision montre toujours le même genre d'émission.

Beaucoup de gens regardent trop la télé et ne peuvent pas s'en passer.

A mon avis il y a trop d'émissions inutiles et idiotes à la télé.

Exercise 40 – Put the following sentences into a negative form:
The word in brackets will tell you the negative form to use.

Je regarde la télé quand il fait beau.	(never)
J'aime regarder les émissions de sports.	(only)
Je regarde les feuilletons tous les jours.	(no longer)
Il y a beaucoup d'émissions intéressantes à la télé.	(not)
J'aime les feuilletons et les films.	(neither nor)

Education and Work

Education and work is another big topic within the Higher programme and we will start off by brainstorming ideas of what should be studied in this topic.

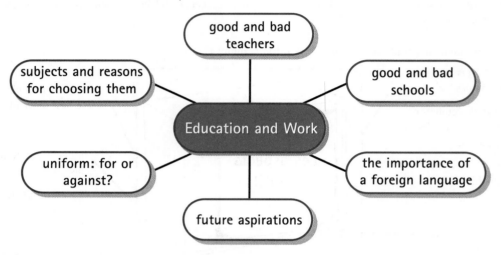

TOPIC 1 School and Teachers – Le Lycée et Les Professeurs

We will start off by looking at some vocabulary which will help you in this section.

Remember to do the 'vocabulary timing game' to help you learn the following words.

General vocabulary

• enseigner	– to teach
• apprendre	– to learn/to teach
• étudier	– to study
• passer un examen	– to sit an exam
• réussir à un examen	– to pass an exam
• échouer à un examen	– to fail an exam

• des activités parascolaires	– extra-curricular activities
• un enseignant	– a teacher
• un professeur	– a teacher
• un surveillant/un pion	– a person (not a teacher) who looks after the pupils during break/lunch, etc.

• un lycée	– a secondary school (after Standard Grades)
• un collège	– a secondary school (up to Standard Grades)
• une école primaire	– a primary school
• un internat	– a boarding school

• prendre une année sabbatique	– to take a year out
• travailler à l'étranger	– to work abroad
• aller à la faculté	– to go to university

Let's now look at the qualities of a good teacher. Here are some ideas that you will be able to use.

The sentences on the following page have all been included on the CD.

- Remember to use your dictionary to look up any words you do not understand.
- All the phrases could be used when preparing a talk or a piece of writing, so choose the ones you feel most comfortable with.
- **Exercise 41** – Try translating them into English.

Un bon prof est celui qui est + adjective

exemple, sérieux
patient
prêt à aider
consciencieux
chaleureux
équitable

(A lot of the adjectives used to discuss good parents could be used again here.)

TRACK 32

Un bon prof est celui qui + verb

exemple, explique tout clairement
apporte l'aide nécessaire
prépare bien ses cours

Un bon prof a + noun

exemple, le sens de l'humour

Remember if you want to talk about bad teachers/un mauvais prof (your favourite topic!) use the negative form.

exemple, un mauvais prof est celui   qui n'est pas patient
qui n'explique rien
qui n'a pas le sens de l'humour

Now let's look at what makes a good school. You will already have a lot of ideas on this but here are just a few to jog your memory.

Feel free to add any ideas you may have.

Un bon lycée est celui qui a + noun

exemple, une atmosphère sympa
un bon taux de réussite aux examens
de la discipline
de bons rapports entre profs et élèves

Un bon lycée est celui où + noun

exemple, les élèves ont envie de réussir
les profs sont disponibles
il n'y a pas de violence

Un bon lycée est celui qui + verb

exemple, signale les absences
protège ses élèves
est bien équipé

As previously said, you may want to talk about a bad school/un mauvais lycée. Once again, you can use the same phrases as above but remember to put them into the negative form,
exemple, un mauvais lycée est celui qui n'a pas une atmosphère sympa
un mauvais lycée est celui où les élèves n'ont pas envie de réussir
un mauvais lycée est celui qui ne signale pas les absences.

This next exercise will help improve your listening skills and allow you to add more vocabulary and phrases to the lists above.

- First read the sentences below.
- Use a dictionary to look up any words you do not understand.
- Remember you will need to look up the infinitive of verbs to find the correct meaning.

TRACK 33

Exercise 42 – Now listen to the interview with Julien and put a tick beside each sentence that Julien agrees with.

Listen two or three times if necessary.

Qu'est-ce qu'un bon prof?

Un bon enseignant ...

est une personne qui aime travailler avec les gens

est juste et équitable avec tout le monde

a un très bon sens de l'humour

ne donne pas trop de devoirs

apporte une aide nécessaire lorsque quelqu'un en a besoin

explique sa matière de façon claire et précise en donnant des exemples.

Qu'est-ce qu'un mauvais prof?

Un mauvais prof ...

est souvent en colère contre ses élèves

donne des examens tous les jours

est toujours très sérieux et sévère

a un *chouchou dans chaque classe

donne seulement des exercices sans les expliquer.

Qu'est-ce qu'une bonne école?

Une bonne école ...

est assez spacieuse

a un personnel compétent qui est toujours prêt à aider

organise des activités spéciales chaque année

implique les élèves dans la vie scolaire

respecte les cultures de tous les élèves

possède du matériel informatique récent

est un endroit sûr où l'on peut se promener sans danger

propose des activités parascolaires intéressantes pour les élèves.

* un chouchou – a teacher's pet

Now check your answers.

You may also wish to read the transcript to see where you had difficulties.

Make a list of any words or expressions that you feel would be useful for preparing a talk or a piece of writing.

Now it's your turn – tell us what you think makes a good teacher and a good school.

Use the phrases you have already heard and seen to help you.

Un bon prof ...

Un mauvais prof ...

Une bonne école ...

We will now look at a somewhat controversial topic at school – uniform.

Everybody has his/her own ideas, but here are a few in French which should be considered.

Before you start, however, you may wish to say whether you wear a uniform or not, e.g.

- Dans mon école on doit/nous devons/il faut porter un uniforme c'est-à-dire + describe your uniform.

- Dans mon école nous ne sommes pas obligés de porter un uniforme.

Let's look at some advantages of wearing uniform. Listen to the CD at the same time to help with your pronunciation.

Les avantages de porter un uniforme

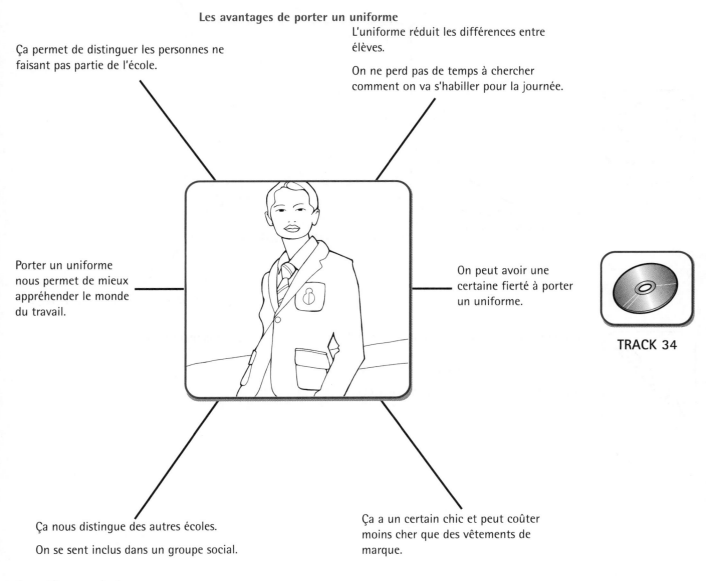

Ça permet de distinguer les personnes ne faisant pas partie de l'école.

L'uniforme réduit les différences entre élèves.

On ne perd pas de temps à chercher comment on va s'habiller pour la journée.

Porter un uniforme nous permet de mieux appréhender le monde du travail.

On peut avoir une certaine fierté à porter un uniforme.

TRACK 34

Ça nous distingue des autres écoles.

On se sent inclus dans un groupe social.

Ça a un certain chic et peut coûter moins cher que des vêtements de marque.

Specific vocabulary
- appréhender   – *to fully appreciate/to apprehend*
- avoir une certaine fierté   – *to take a certain pride in*

Now let's look at some disadvantages. These are on the CD to help you with your pronunciation.

Les inconvénients de porter un uniforme

On perd son individualité.

On s'habille tous de la même façon.

Ce n'est pas confortable pour travailler.

En été on a trop chaud et en hiver on a trop froid.

TRACK 35

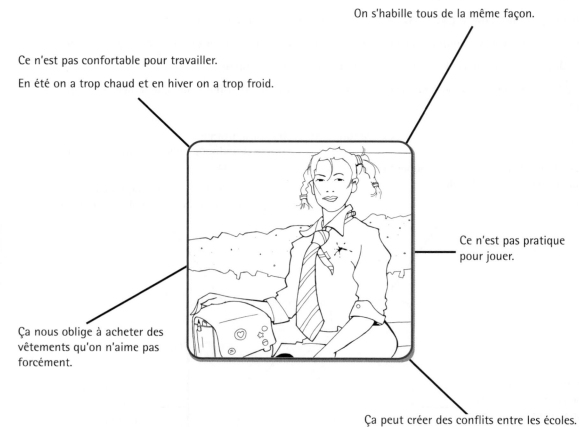

Ce n'est pas pratique pour jouer.

Ça nous oblige à acheter des vêtements qu'on n'aime pas forcément.

Ça peut créer des conflits entre les écoles.

Exercise 43 – For both the advantages and disadvantages, practise translating the phrases into English.

Alors et toi, es-tu pour ou contre? – Are you for or against?

Moi je suis pour/contre l'uniforme parce que ...

You will of course have to explain the reasons why you have chosen certain subjects, so it is important at this time to revise subjects.

However, please do not list all the subjects you have done, but choose one or two that you feel you can give a good explanation as to your choice. It goes without saying that French or some language will always win you some 'brownie points'.

Here are some different ways of saying why you have chosen certain subjects.

- Read the sentences below.
- Use your dictionary to look up any words you do not understand.
- **Exercise 44** – Practise your translation skills by translating the sentences into English, ensuring that they make sense. Be careful with your tenses.

Before listening, you could try reading the sentences aloud for pronunciation practice.

- Je m'intéresse beaucoup à la musique et donc j'ai décidé de l'étudier cette année.
- J'ai décidé d'étudier le sport cette année car je suis très sportif(ve) et un jour j'aimerais être professeur de sport.
- J'ai choisi l'informatique car je pense que de nos jours, il est très important de savoir bien maîtriser la technologie.
- Je me passionne pour la lecture et la poésie alors j'ai choisi l'anglais pour approfondir mes connaissances.
- J'ai choisi les maths cette année car je trouve que c'est indispensable pour la vie de tous les jours.
- J'ai choisi les maths et la physique car je trouve que ce sont deux matières fondamentales pour mieux expliquer le monde qui nous entoure.

TRACK 36

Now listen to the CD to improve on any pronunciation difficulties you may have.

Now it's your turn. Write a couple of sentences saying why you have chosen a particular subject(s).

Reasons for studying a foreign language – l'importance d'étudier une langue étrangère

Exercise 45a – Listen to the CD and complete the sentences choosing from the phrases below.

If you're feeling confident try not to look at the phrases first, but use them to check your answers.

Listen again and practise your pronunciation of the more difficult words.

Bonne chance!

TRACK 37

- Je trouve que c'est très important d'étudier une langue étrangère car ...
- Le fait d'étudier une langue étrangère nous aide ...
- Une langue étrangère nous permet de ...
- J'ai choisi le français car je veux ...
- A mon avis, les langues étrangères sont ...

Phrases to complete the sentences above:

- étudier les langues à la faculté
- on devient plus tolérant envers d'autres cultures
- communiquer avec les gens de différents pays
- indispensables pour l'Union Européenne
- à mieux comprendre notre propre langue.

Exercise 45b – Practise your translation skills by translating the above sentences into English.

Use a dictionary if necessary.

TOPIC 4 Future Aspirations – Aspirations Futures

Once again we will brainstorm ideas concerning this topic.

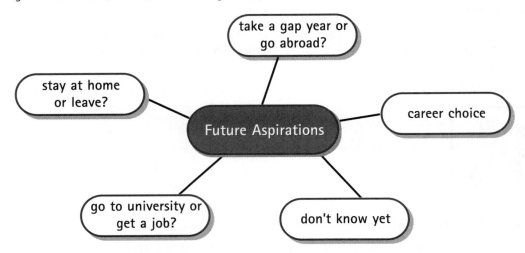

As we will now look at future aspirations, it seems like the perfect time to have a quick reminder of both the future and conditional tenses.

Future tense – a quick revision

Basically take the infinitive form of the verb and add the following endings:

je	-ai	nous	-ons
tu	-as	vous	-ez
il/elle/on	-a	ils/elles	-ont

e.g. quitter – to leave

je quitterai	– *I will leave*	nous quitterons	– *we will leave*
tu quitteras	– *you will leave*	vous quitterez	– *you will leave*
il/elle/on quittera	– *he/she/we will leave*	ils/elles quitteront	– *they will leave*

Watch verbs which end in -re as you must drop the -e before adding the endings, for example:

attendr(e)	- *to wait for*	j'attendrai	- *I will wait*

Be careful!

When using when ('quand' in French), the first clause also has to be in the future tense, although it would be the present tense in English.

Look at the following examples.

Example 1

Quand je quitterai l'école, j'irai à l'etranger.

If this were to be translated literally it would be:

When I <u>will</u> leave school, I will go abroad.

However, it would be more natural in English to translate it as:

When I leave school, I will go abroad.

Example 2

Quand j'aurai fini mes devoirs, je jouerai au foot.

If this were to be translated literally it would be:

When I <u>will have finished</u> my homework, I will play football.

Once again this would need to be changed to:

When I have finished my homework, I will play football.

These examples show the importance of understanding the different tenses both in English and French.

When translating, you need to ensure that you use the correct tense and that your English makes perfect sense.

The conditional tense

We have already looked at the conditional tense, but here is a quick reminder.

aimer – *to like*

j'aimerais	– *I would like*	nous aimerions	– *we would like*
tu aimerais	– *you would like*	vous aimeriez	– *you would like*
il/elle/on aimerait	– *he/she/we would like*	ils/elles aimeraient	– *they would like*

Exceptions

There are of course exceptions in both the conditional tenses and future tenses. However the endings remain the same. Here are a few examples in the third person singular (the 'il' form).

Exercise 46 – Try to complete the table for the last four verbs.

Infinitive	Future	Conditional
être	il sera	il serait
avoir	il aura	il aurait
aller	il ira	il irait
faire	il fera	il ferait
savoir	il saura	il saurait
pouvoir	....	....
vouloir	....	....
voir	....	....
venir	....	....

It is very important that you know these verbs and are able to use them with ease.

Remember!

Add the imperfect endings to the infinitive.

Test yourself!

Exercise 47 – Practise your knowledge of future and conditional tenses by trying out the multiple-choice quiz.

> **TIPS** to help improve reading and translating skills
>
> - First read each phrase or sentence.
> - Decide what the words mean.
> - Use a dictionary to look up the words you do not understand.
> - Check the grammar and the structure of the sentence.
> - Think about translating skills – does your English translation make sense?

1 What is the future **'ils'** form of 'avoir' meaning 'they will have'?

   a avoiront

   b ont

   c auront

   d avont

2 What is the conditional **'vous'** form of 'faire' meaning 'you would do'?

   a ferez

   b ferais

   c feriez

   d faites

3 What is the future **'nous'** form of 'savoir' meaning 'we will know'?

   a saurons

   b savons

   c saurions

   d savoirons

4 Which sentence is incorrect?

   a Je n'aimerais pas vivre à l'étranger.

   b Il n'irait jamais en France.

   c Ils aimerait vivre ensemble.

   d Je ne quitterais jamais l'Ecosse.

5 Which of the following sentences is best translated by 'When I leave school, I will go to Spain'?

   a Quand je quitte l'école, je vais en Espagne.

   b Quand je quitterai l'école, je vais en Espagne.

   c Quand je quitterais l'école, j'irais en Espagne.

   d Quand je quitterai l'école, j'irai en Espagne.

6 Which of the following sentences means 'I will never be a maths teacher'?

   a Je ne sera jamais professeur de maths.

   b Je ne serai jamais professeur de maths.

   c Je etreai jamais professeur de maths.

   d Je ne serais jamais professeur de maths.

7 What is the best translation for the following sentence? 'Quand j'aurai fini mes études, j'irai à l'étranger.'

    a   When I will have finished my studies I will go abroad.

    b   When I have finished my studies I will go abroad.

    c   When I would have finished my studies, I will go abroad.

    d   When I finish my studies, I will go with a stranger.

8 Which of the following sentences means 'When I have passed all my exams, I will go to university'?

    a   Quand j'aurai passé tous mes examens, j'irai à la fac.

    b   Quand j'aurai réussis à tous mes examens, j'irai à la fac.

    c   Quand je passe mes examens, j'irai à la fac.

    d   Quand je réussis à tous mes examens, j'irai à la fac.

 **Bravo! Tu as réussi!**

Check your answers at the back to see how well you did.

The correct answers have been given to all the incorrect sentences used in this quiz.

All these correct sentences can be used for both speaking and writing practice. Select the sentences that you feel most confident with and try to use them for these purposes.

Future aspirations

Remember!
Revise jobs

What are your future aspirations? What would you like to do later in life?

Here are some ideas:

- Read the sentences below.

- Check the meanings of any words you do not understand in your dictionary.

- Pay particular attention to the tenses, remembering to look up the infinitives of any verbs.

- **Exercise 48** – Practise your translation skills by translating the sentences into English.

- All of the sentences below can be used when preparing a talk or a piece of writing on this topic.

TRACK 38

You can also listen to them on the CD to help with your pronunciation.

Go to university? – Aller à la faculté/à l'université?

- Quand je quitterai l'école, j'aimerais aller à la fac pour étudier + subject(s) car je veux être + job.

- Si je réussis à mes examens, j'irai à l'université de Glasgow afin d'étudier le droit.

Go abroad? – Aller à l'étranger?

(refer back to life in the town and country section)

- Un jour j'aimerais vivre à l'étranger car je m'intéresse beaucoup à d'autres cultures.

- Quand je quitterai l'école, j'aimerais aller en France pour mieux connaître les traditions de ce pays et améliorer mon français.

A gap year? – Prendre une année sabbatique?

- Quand je quitterai l'école, j'aimerais prendre une année sabbatique pour me reposer.

- L'année prochaine, quand j'aurai quitté l'école, j'aimerais prendre une année sabbatique et faire du volontariat.

Look for a job? – Chercher du travail?

- Après mon baccalauréat, j'aimerais commencer tout de suite à travailler pour gagner de l'argent.

- Quand je quitterai l'école, j'aimerais trouver un travail car je veux mon propre appartement et mon indépendance.

Stay at home or leave? – Rester à la maison ou partir?

- Je préférerais rester à la maison pendant mes études car on y a tout le confort pour étudier et ça me permettrait de dépenser moins d'argent.

- J'aimerais aller à la fac dans une autre ville parce que je veux profiter de la vie d'étudiant.

- Dès que je trouverai du travail, je déménagerai car je ne m'entends pas très bien avec mes parents.

- Moi, je resterai à la maison le plus longtemps possible car je suis proche de ma famille et j'ai un peu peur de vivre loin d'elle.

Don't know? – Je ne sais pas?

- Moi, je ne sais pas ce que je veux faire quand je quitterai l'école. D'ailleurs ça me fait un peu peur.

- En ce moment je ne sais pas encore ce que je ferai lorsque je quitterai l'école mais ça ne m'inquiète pas trop.

Now it's your turn.

Write a couple of sentences saying what your future aspirations are.

Focus on Reading/Translation

Let's practise some reading skills.

Exercise 49 – On the next two pages you will see five extracts of people talking about their present education and future aspirations!

Before you read them, look at the eight questions below.

1 Who wants to work with computers?

2 Who doesn't know what they want to do?

3 Who wants to become a professional swimmer?

4 Who feels that languages are very important in the workplace?

5 Who will 'no doubt, stay at home during their studies'?

6 Who loves history?

7 Who really wants to go to university next year?

8 Who says 'unfortunately, I don't like studying'?

Before reading the five passages think about the French sentences and words you are looking for to be able to answer the questions.

Make a list of these next to each question.

Now quickly read over the passages and see how many of the questions you can answer!

Now read again and fill in the gaps.

Sylvie

En ce moment je suis en terminale et j'étudie pour mon baccalauréat. Comme je trouve que les langues étrangères sont très importantes dans le monde du travail, je prête beaucoup d'attention à ces matières. J'aimerais aller à la fac dans un an mais l'an prochain je veux aller en Angleterre afin d'améliorer mon anglais et d'apprendre plus de choses sur la culture britannique.

Thomas

Je suis dans ma dernière année à l'école et je vais bientôt passer mes examens. Je me passionne beaucoup pour le sport, surtout la natation et j'aimerais un jour devenir professionnel.

Je crois que je chercherai un petit boulot à mi-temps l'an prochain pour me permettre de payer mes cours de natation et de m'entraîner plus souvent.

Christine

En ce moment je prépare mes examens que je passerai dans deux mois. J'adore l'histoire car ça nous apprend beaucoup sur nos ancêtres et sur la vie d'aujourd'hui.

En ce moment je ne sais vraiment pas ce que je veux faire l'an prochain, mais il va falloir que je me décide bientôt car ça commence à créer des tensions dans ma famille.

Christophe

Je suis dans ma dernière année à l'école où j'étudie 5 matières. Je suis très fort en informatique et un jour j'aimerais travailler dans ce domaine.

Malheureusement je n'aime pas trop étudier et je crois que l'année prochaine je prendrai une année sabbatique pour me retrouver et réfléchir à ce que je veux faire dans l'avenir.

Julien

Je suis en terminale et prépare mon baccalauréat. Comme je veux absolument aller à la fac l'an prochain pour étudier le droit il faut que je réussisse cette année. Les études de droit durent sept ans alors je resterai sans doute à la maison pour finir mes études car c'est plus pratique et ça coûte trop cher de vivre tout seul.

Translation practice

In your final exam, you will be asked to translate a small passage.

Exercise 50 – To give you some practice of this, try translating the following passage by Christine.

Remember to pay particular attention to your tenses and English.

En ce moment je prépare mes examens que je passerai dans deux mois. J'adore l'histoire car ça nous apprend beaucoup sur nos ancêtres et sur la vie d'aujourd'hui.

En ce moment je ne sais vraiment pas ce que je veux faire l'an prochain, mais il va falloir que je me décide bientôt car ça commence à créer des tensions dans ma famille.

Things to watch

en ce moment	– at the moment/at present/currently
je prépare	– although there is no extra word for 'for' in French, this is best translated by 'I am preparing for'
que	– means 'which' here
je passerai	– future tense and 'passer un examen' means to sit an exam therefore the best translation would be 'I will take/sit'.
ça nous apprend	– remember apprendre can also mean teach. Please do not write 'that learns us' – the best translation is 'it teaches us'.
il va falloir que je me décide	– this is a difficult construction and translated literally would read 'it is going to be necessary that I decide myself'. Obviously this does not make sense in English and the best translation would be 'I am going to have to decide/ I will need to decide or make my mind up' (se decider).
ça commence	– Which form of the present tense fits better: begins/does begin/is beginning? Here the continuous present 'is beginning' fits best.

Test yourself

Exercise 51 – What do the following words mean?

- enseigner

- un lycée

- apprendre

- un pion

- échouer à un examen

- passer un examen

- les matières

- les langues étrangères

Exercise 52 – Translate the following sentences into English:

Un bon prof est quelqu'un qui écoute les élèves.

Un bon prof est toujours équitable et disponible.

Une bonne école a rarement des problèmes de discipline.

Une bonne école a une atmosphère chaleureuse.

Je m'intéresse beaucoup aux langues étrangères.

Je me passionne pour la musique.

Cette année j'étudie le français car je trouve que les langues étrangères sont importantes pour ma carrière.

Exercise 53 – Look at the following sentences and correct the word underlined:

Quand je quitterais l'école j'aimerais être avocat.

Un bon prof est celui qui expliquet tout clairement.

Un mauvais prof est celui qui est trop sévères et stricts.

Je ne sait pas si je veut aller à la fac.

Une bon école est une endroit ou on se sent en sécurité.

Introduction to Directed Writing

As the name suggests this part of the exam is a directed task and will require you to write an account of a trip or an exchange visit to France.

To do well in this exercise, you must ensure that:

* You write between 150–180 words.
* Your piece of writing is accurate and makes sense.
* You answer each bullet point accurately and efficiently.
* The standard of vocabulary is of Higher Level.

Although the scenarios differ to a certain degree and generally you will only be asked to give information on six bullet points, you should be prepared to write about any of the following:

* When and where you went and for how long.
* Who you went with.
* How you travelled and what you thought of the trip.
* Where you stayed and what you thought of the accommodation.
* Information about your job and duties.
* Information about the school and town.
* What you thought of the people – colleagues, school teachers or pupils.
* What you did in your free time and in the evenings.
* What you thought of the food.
* Evaluation of the trip.

Don't panic!

You are already familiar with a lot of the vocabulary and grammatical structures required for this piece of writing.

This section will therefore help to reinforce what you already know and prepare you for any eventuality in this part of the exam.

Read all the phrases you see in this section carefully. Try using your dictionary to help you with any words you do not understand. Remember to use it carefully, however.

You can also practise your translation skills by translating some of the sentences into English.

As the Directed Writing requires you to write about a past event, you will be predominately using the Perfect and the Imperfect tenses.

Oh no, not grammar again!

Well yes. Grammar is essential to ensure that your sentences are correctly structured and make sense. Just think of the benefits that a good grammar base will bring, not only to the Directed Writing section, but to all your pieces of writing.

The Perfect Tense

Let's start with a little reminder on how we form the perfect tense.

Easy!

Present part of 'avoir'

j'ai
tu as
il/elle/on a
nous avons
vous avez
ils/elles ont

Regular 'er', 'ir' and 're' verbs

Infinitive	Past participle	Example
–er (manger)	–é (mangé)	j'ai mangé (I ate, I have eaten)
–ir (finir)	–i (fini)	tu as/vous avez fini (you finished/you have finished)
–re (vendre)	–u (vendu)	il a/ils ont vendu (he/they sold, he has/they have sold)

Here's the bad news: some verbs have irregular past participles, e.g. lire, faire, boire, etc. They have to be learned and can be found in the verb section of your dictionary.

To make French more of a challenge some verbs also take the verb 'être' instead of 'avoir'. Many of you will know rhymes and poems to help you remember these, but if not as a general rule of thumb most verbs of movement and all reflexive verbs take 'être'.

The rule for these verbs is as in the above table but instead of 'avoir' use the correct form of 'être'.

Example: I went = je suis allé(e)
He arrived = il est arrivé
We got up = on s'est levé, nous nous sommes levé(e)s

TIPS for forming the perfect tense

- Perfect Tense with avoir = 2 things to check:
  1) correct part of avoir
  2) correct form of past participle
- Perfect Tense with être = 3 things to check:
  1) correct part of être
  2) correct form of past participle
  3) correct agreement (-, -e, -s, -es)

Remember!
One further complication with être verbs. The past participle must agree with the subject (just like adjectives) so add an extra 'e' for feminine, an 's' for plural and an 'es' for feminine plural.

The Imperfect Tense

You will use this past tense mainly to **describe** what the journey/town/people, etc. were like and to say what you used to do/did **regularly** – each day/in your free time/at weekends.

To form this tense is easy, promise!

All you need to do is:

- Look at the 'nous' form of the verb in the present tense.
- Remove the 'ons'.
- Add on the following endings – ais, ais, ait, ions, iez, aient.

Example

Infinitive	Present Tense
aller	nous allons

Imperfect

j'allais	nous allions
tu allais	vous alliez
il/elle/on allait	ils/elles allaient

'Ah, but no exceptions?' I hear you say.

But of course! This is French!

You've guessed it – the verb 'être' is an exception to the rule and again has to be learned.

One piece of good news, however. It does have the regular imperfect endings.

être

j'étais	nous étions
tu étais	vous étiez
il/elle/on était	ils/elles étaient

Now let's see if you have been reading attentively and have understood these simple grammatical rules. Try out the grammar quiz below.

Bonne chance!

The Grammar Quiz

Exercise 54

1 Which of the following is incorrect?

   a   J'ai passé deux semaines en France

   b   L'an dernier nous avons passé un mois en France

   c   Pendant les grandes vacances nous sommes allé en France

   d   L'été dernier on est allé en France pour quatre semaines

2 True or false? All French verbs take the verb 'avoir' in the perfect tense?

3 Which of the following past participles would you use to complete this sentence?

   Elles sont ... à dix heures du soir

   a   arrivée

   b   arrivé

   c   arrivés

   d   arrivées

4 True or false? The imperfect tense has no exceptions to the rule?

5 Which of the following sentences is correct?

   a   l'hôtel se trouvais en face d'une grande place

   b   nous se promenions tous les jours

   c   la chambre donnaient sur un lac

   d   l'hôtel était situé en pleine ville

6 Which of the following past participles is incorrect?

    a boire – bois

    b avoir – eu

    c passer – passé

    d faire – fait

Here are some verb phrases, in their infinitive form, which you will be able to use during your piece of writing.

Practise putting them into the imperfect or perfect tenses.

* = irregular past participle   ** = takes the verb être

passer une semaine en France	– *to spend a week in France*
avoir de la chance de passer ...*	– *to be lucky to spend ...*
aller en France**	– *to go to France*
faire un voyage/un échange scolaire*	– *to go on a trip/school exchange*
prendre le train/l'avion/l'Eurostar*	– *to take the train/plane/the Eurostar*
quitter Glasgow	– *to leave Glasgow*
loger dans une auberge de jeunesse	– *to stay in a youth hostel*
faire du camping*	– *to go camping*
partager une chambre	– *to share a room*
se trouver à...**	– *to be situated at*
prendre les repas/le dîner*	– *to have meals/dinner*
visiter les monuments	– *to visit monuments*
faire des excursions*	– *to go on excursions*
faire du shopping/les courses*	– *to go shopping/food shopping*
acheter des cadeaux/des souvenirs	– *to buy presents/souvenirs*
faire du lèche-vitrine*	– *to go window shopping*
profiter du beau temps	– *to take advantage of the good weather*
faire une promenade en bateau mouche*	– *to go for a trip on a pleasure boat*
aller au restaurant**	– *to go to a restaurant*
passer une journée à la plage	– *to spend a day on the beach*
prendre un verre sur la terrasse*	– *to have a drink on the terrace*
se baigner**	– *to go swimming*
nager	– *to swim*
jouer au volley, etc.	– *to play volley ball, etc.*
lire*	– *to read*
bronzer	– *to sunbathe*
faire du ski/de la natation, etc.*	– *to go skiing/swimming, etc.*
bien s'amuser**	– *to really enjoy oneself*
s'ennuyer (à mourir)**	– *to be bored (to death)*
se coucher tôt/tard**	– *to go to bed early/late*
se lever de bonne heure**	– *to get up early*
apprendre une langue*	– *to learn a language*
voir un nouveau pays*	– *to see a new country*

We will now look at the different bullet points in turn and think of ways of approaching each one so that you are fully prepared and can transfer all the ideas to any situation.

One of the most predictable bullet points will be:

When and where you went and for how long

Let's brainstorm this and think of what you will need to know:

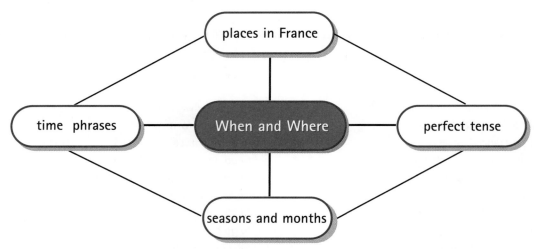

As you can see from the above diagram it is important that you know vocabulary for time phrases, e.g. last year, etc, seasons and months and different places in France. These all then have to be linked together using the perfect tense.

Try to think of some expressions that you already know under each of the headings:

- Places in France (include in the south, north, the Alps, etc.)

- Seasons and months

- Time expressions (last year, during, a year ago, etc.)

Now using the perfect tense try to link your expressions to produce some sentences explaining when and where you went.

Here are some extra ideas that you could use:

- L'été dernier, j'ai eu la chance de passer deux semaines en France.

- Pendant les vacances de Pâques/Noël/été je suis allé(e) à Lyon en France.

- L'année dernière, pendant les grandes vacances, je suis allé(e) à Perpignan dans le sud-ouest de la France.

- L'an dernier au mois de juin/août/décembre, nous sommes allés à Grenoble dans les Alpes.

- Nous avons passé deux semaines extraordinaires ...

  à Paris en France
  à Concarneau en Bretagne, au nord-ouest de la France
  à Nîmes en Provence.

The next bullet point you may have to address is:

Who you went with

You are most likely to say you went with either a friend, a member of your family, with the school or alone.

Here are some ideas:

- Il y avait vingt élèves dans le groupe.

- Nous étions une vingtaine.

- Deux professeurs de français nous ont accompagnés/accompagnaient.

- L'an dernier on a participé à un échange scolaire.

- C'était un voyage d'études.

- Je suis allé(e) avec ma mère, ma sœur, ma famille, ma meilleure amie, mon meilleur ami, etc ...

- Un de mes amis et moi, nous sommes allé(e)s.

- Je suis allé(e) en France tout(e) seul(e).

Now you are feeling confident with the first two bullet points, let's try a little exercise.

Exercise 55 – Listen to the CD provided and write down the six sentences about when and where you went and who you went with.

Remember to pay attention to your tenses and the spelling.

Check your answers by looking at the transcript.

You could also listen to the CD again and practise your pronunciation by reading the sentences along with the CD.

TRACK 39

Bravo! Tu as réussi!

Now that you have a lot of different phrases to be able to start your piece of writing confidently, we will move on.

The next quite predictable bullet point is all about:

(How you travelled and what you thought of the trip)

Once again we will brainstorm this point and think about the vocabulary and grammar we need to know to answer accurately and fully.

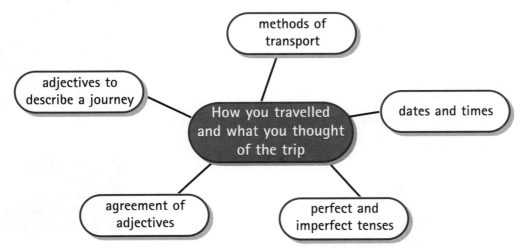

Again it is important to know the vocabulary for the above points and link them together using the correct tense.

Try to think of vocabulary and expressions you might use for the following headings:

- Different methods of transport

- Times and dates of departure and arrival

- Adjectives to describe the trip

Directed Writing

Remember!
voyager + en
prendre + le/la/l'

Remember!
You must make adjectives agree in French.
Unless the word finishes in 'e' or 's', add an 'e' for feminine, an 's' for plural and an 'es' for feminine plural.

Here are some more ideas:

- On a voyagé en car/en avion/en train.
- On a pris le train/l'avion/le car/le ferry.
- Nous sommes partis en train de Glasgow le samedi matin et sommes arrivés en France le dimanche après-midi.
- On a quitté Glasgow le lundi après-midi à bord d'un avion qui nous a amenés jusqu'à Paris.
- On est parti dans un car qu'on a pu utiliser pendant tout le séjour pour visiter tous les monuments célèbres de Paris.
- Le voyage était long et ennuyeux.
- J'avais peur dans le ferry parce que la mer était très agitée.
- Le voyage a passé très vite car on a regardé un film dans l'avion.
- Les professeurs ont organisé des quiz dans le car alors on s'est bien amusé pendant le voyage.

Now let's look at the next bullet point.

Where you stayed and what you thought of the accommodation

We will break this down into two points.

Firstly where you stayed

As previously said try to write a little about the area in which you stayed. However if you do this make sure you know a little about this area so that it makes sense.

Do not start saying 'during our time in Lyon, we went to the beach everyday'.

Lyon is a long way from the beach and although possible, it would be highly improbable that you would do this if you spent time in Lyon.

To help you to ensure that you know a little about the different places in France, we have provided you with some phrases about your accommodation and its situation in four different areas of France.

Paris ...

On a passé deux semaines dans une auberge qui se trouvait dans le 7ème arrondissement près du Quartier Latin.

L'hôtel se trouvait à cinq minutes de la Tour Eiffel.

L'hôtel donnait sur la Seine.

La maison de mon correspondant était située à côté des Champs Elysées.

Dans les Alpes ...

L'hôtel se trouvait au centre d'une station de ski. C'était vraiment génial.

On a logé dans une auberge qui donnait sur de hautes montagnes couvertes de neige.

En Bretagne ...

L'hôtel se trouvait à cinquante mètres de la plage. C'était super.

La maison de mon correspondant se trouvait à vingt kilomètres du Mont St Michel.

L'auberge de jeunesse donnait sur la mer. C'était super.

En Provence ...

L'hôtel se trouvait en pleine Garrigue qui est une région très sauvage et isolée.

Nous avons campé dans un petit village provençal à une demi-heure d'un lac où on se baignaient tous les jours.

L'auberge de jeunesse donnait sur des vignobles.

Now we look at what you thought of the accommodation

Once again you should already know a lot of adjectives to describe your accommodation.

Here are some adjectives that you may wish to use:

Try the 'vocabulary timing game' to help you learn the adjectives.

L'auberge de jeunesse/l'hôtel/la maison de mon correspondant était ...

Remember!
The adjective rule – look back to page 13 if you need a little reminder!

- grand(e)/petit(e)   – *big/small*
- moderne   – *modern*
- vieux/vieille *   – *old*
- confortable/peu confortable – *comfortable/uncomfortable*
- spacieux/spacieuse *   – *spacious*
- joli(e)   – *pretty, nice*
- laid(e)   – *ugly*
- bien décoré(e)   – *well decorated*
- de mauvais goût   – *bad taste*
- propre   – *clean*
- sale   – *dirty*
- beau/belle   – *beautiful*

* for adjectives ending in 'x' you would normally change them to 'se' in the feminine. Vieux, however, changes to vieille and beau changes to belle.

You may wish to elaborate and add some information about the room you stayed in:

- J'ai partagé une chambre avec (trois filles/deux garçons/mes copains).

- J'avais la chance d'avoir (ma propre chambre/une chambre à moi).

- Je me suis vraiment senti(e) (à l'aise/comme chez moi).

Giving opinions is another good way of expressing your feelings about where you stayed. These can also be used for many different contexts and situations.

- C'était super/génial/excellent.

- C'était vraiment bien.

- C'était nul/pénible/affreux.

On the CD you will hear four people describing their journey and their accommodation.

TRACK 40

Exercise 56a – Write down as many adjectives and opinions as you can hear for each one.

Now before you listen, again try to fill in the blanks.

1 L'été dernier je suis allé en Bretagne dans le nord de la France avec l'école. Nous avons pris le car jusqu'à Douvres et puis le ferry jusqu'à Calais. Ensuite le car nous a amené jusqu'à notre destination en Bretagne. Le voyage était très .... et .... et dans le ferry j'ai été malade. C'était .... Une fois arrivés, nous sommes allés à l'auberge de jeunesse qui se trouvait dans un petit village. Elle était .... mais vraiment .... En plus je devais partager la chambre avec mon meilleur ami. C'était .... et on s'est bien ....

2 Pendant les vacances de Pâques, j'ai eu la chance de trouver un travail dans un hôtel à Paris en France. J'ai pris l'avion à l'aéroport de Glasgow le samedi matin et je suis arrivé à Paris à midi. Le voyage était .... et très .... car c'était la première fois que je prenais l'avion. Une fois arrivé à Paris, j'ai pris le métro pour aller dans le seizième arrondissement où se trouvait mon hôtel. Le métro n'était pas .... mais il était très .... J'avais un peu peur. L'hôtel, par contre, était très .... et .... Il était vraiment .... car il se trouvait à cinq minutes de la Tour Eiffel. C'était .... J'avais ma propre chambre qui était vraiment .... et très bien .... Je me suis senti tout de suite à l'aise.

3 Il y a un an, pendant les vacances de Noël, j'ai participé à un échange scolaire. Nous sommes allés à Grenoble dans les Alpes pour une semaine et c'était .... On est parti de Glasgow en train le dimanche matin pour arriver à Grenoble le lundi à midi. Le voyage était .... car c'était très .... et il faisait froid dans les wagons. A la gare de Grenoble les familles d'accueil nous attendaient pour nous amener chez elles. C'était .... de leur part. La maison de ma famille d'accueil était .... C'était comme un chalet suisse et il y avait une belle vue sur les Alpes. C'était .... La maison était .... et .... et j'avais même une chambre à moi.

4 Pendant les grandes vacances je suis allée en Provence, en France avec l'école. Nous étions vingt élèves et trois professeurs. Nous avons quitté Glasgow en car à une heure du matin et puis nous avons pris l'Eurostar pour arriver en France le lendemain à deux heures de l'après-midi. Ensuite on a continué notre voyage en car jusqu'à notre destination en Provence. Le voyage ne m'a pas semblé très .... parce que le car était .... et qu'on a pu dormir. L'Eurostar était très .... aussi. Nous avons logé dans une auberge de jeunesse en Provence qui se trouvait en pleine campagne. L'auberge était très .... et assez .... En plus les chambres étaient très .... et .... On n'était pas très .... de notre logement.

Now check your answers.

Remember that you could use or adapt any of the above passages in your own Directed Writing piece.

Exercise 56b – You could also practise translating the passages to improve your translation skills.

Bravo! Tu as réussi!

Information about your job and duties

You may be asked to say what job you had while in France. As this will probably be in the service industry, you will not be required to know every different type of job.

Here are the most common.

J'ai travaillé comme ...

- femme/valet de chambre   – *chamber maid*
- serveur(se)   – *waiter (ess)*
- barman   – *barman*
- réceptionniste   – *receptionist*

You will also be required to talk about the duties you had.

Let's take each job in turn and think of some examples.

Here are a few ideas.

Femme/valet de chambre

Je devais nettoyer les chambres des clients, faire les lits et remplir les minibars. De temps en temps je leur apportais le petit déjeuner.

J'étais responsable du nettoyage des chambres des clients et du service du petit déjeuner.

Serveur(se)

Je devais prendre les commandes des clients, les servir et débarrasser les tables.

Je devais mettre les tables et accueillir les clients en arrivant. A la fin du service je débarrassais les tables.

J'étais responsable du service du déjeuner et du dîner.

Barman

Je devais prendre les commandes des clients et leur servir à boire.

Je devais toujours être poli(e)/souriant(e)/agréable.

Réceptionniste

Je devais accueillir les clients, les enregistrer et leur donner la clef de leur chambre.

Je devais répondre au téléphone pour prendre les réservations.

De temps en temps je traduisais pour les clients qui ne parlaient pas français.

Notice the frequent use of the imperfect form of 'devoir' here 'je devais', meaning 'I had to'.

This is always followed by the infinitive of the verb.

Information about the school and town

The next bullet point you may have to address is information about the school or town.

You will already be familiar with a lot of the vocabulary here having used it when talking about your home area in the **Lifestyles** theme, and when talking about your school in **Education and Work**.

Refer back to these two topics to refresh your memory and for any extra ideas.

We will therefore only briefly look at this particular bullet point.

L'école – the school

- Tout était très bizarre/étrange pour moi.
- Les cours commençaient à huit heures et finissaient vers dix-sept heures.
- La pause déjeuner durait une heure et demie et on mangeait à la cantine. On prenait une entrée, un plat principal et soit du fromage soit un dessert.
- C'était une expérience tout à fait différente.
- Tous les cours étaient donnés en français, bien sûr. Au début c'était difficile, mais au bout de quelques jours je me sentais comme un poisson dans l'eau.
- L'école était plus grande/petite que notre école et beaucoup plus moderne/vieille.

Je me sentais comme un poisson dans l'eau – I felt like a fish in water.

La ville – the town

- La ville était très jolie avec beaucoup de cafés où on buvait et discutait à leurs terrasses.
- La ville était très grande et on n'a pas eu le temps de tout visiter.
- La ville était petite et charmante avec de beaux bâtiments anciens. C'était vraiment joli.
- C'était une ville très industrielle et donc pas très jolie.
- Il y avait beaucoup de magasins dans la ville où j'ai acheté beaucoup de cadeaux pour ma famille.

What you thought of the people

You will most definitely have to say what you thought about the people in France. This of course could be referring to your colleagues, the people you stayed with, the teacher and pupils in the school or quite simply the French in general.

Once again, we will only discuss this bullet point briefly as you will already be very familiar with the vocabulary needed to discuss this from earlier topics.

Refer back to '**Family and Friends**' and '**Education and Work**' sections to refresh your memory.

Here are some general phrases that could be used to say how you got on with the different people.

- Mes collègues étaient tous très gentils et m'ont beaucoup aidé(e) dans mon travail.
- Je me suis très bien entendu(e) avec mes collègues de travail. Ils étaient tous très sympa et compréhensifs.
- J'ai beaucoup aimé la famille de mon/ma correspondant(e).
- Tout le monde était très accueillant et je me suis vraiment senti(e) comme chez moi.
- Je me suis très bien amusé(e) avec mon/ma correspondant(e). On avait les mêmes goûts pour tout.
- Tous les profs et les élèves étaient vraiment sympa et m'ont fait vraiment sentir comme chez moi.
- Tout le monde était vraiment accueillant. Ils étaient tous très intéressés par ma vie en Ecosse et les différences entre nos deux cultures.

All the above sentences can be used to talk about all the different people you met.

If you want to say you didn't like the people, just use the negative form.

Reading practice

Exercise 57 – Read the three passages and answer the True/False questions that follow.

TIPS for reading

- Read the True/False questions first to have a general picture.
- Think about the French words you should be looking out for.
- Read all the extracts right through.
- Try to answer some of the questions.
- Go back to the extracts and look up the words in the dictionary that you are unsure of and that you think are important.
- Now go back and try to answer the rest of the questions.

True or False

1 Stéphanie worked as a chamber maid.

   She did not get on with her colleagues.

   She really improved her French.

   She and her colleagues went to coffee shops before going to work.

2 Christophe went to France with friends.

   He had his own room.

   He thought the family were really welcoming.

   He thought the town was quite big and pretty.

3 Thomas went on a school exchange.

   He found the school smaller and more modern than his school.

   He found that the people were very friendly and kind.

   He thought that there was a lot to do in the town.

Reading Extracts

Stéphanie

L'an dernier j'ai travaillé comme serveuse dans un hôtel à Grenoble. J'étais responsable des commandes des clients et du service du déjeuner. Je me suis très bien entendue avec mes collègues. Ils étaient vraiment gentils et m'ont énormément aidé avec le travail et la langue, et par conséquent j'ai beaucoup amélioré mon français. La ville de Grenoble était très jolie avec beaucoup de cafés où on buvait un verre après le travail.

Christophe

L'été dernier je suis allé en France où j'ai passé deux semaines chez mon correspondant. Sa maison n'était pas très grande alors je n'avais pas ma propre chambre. Sa famille était très accueillante et on a fait beaucoup de choses ensemble. Comme la ville n'était ni très jolie ni très grande, on faisait beaucoup d'excursions dans les environs et une fois on est allé à Paris.

Thomas

Le mois de mai dernier j'ai participé à un échange scolaire avec l'école. Nous sommes allés en France pendant deux semaines. L'école en France n'était pas aussi grande que mon école en Ecosse et elle était très vieille aussi. La famille d'accueil était super accueillante et vraiment gentille et je me suis senti vraiment comme chez moi. Le seul inconvénient était qu'il n'y avait pas grand chose à faire dans la ville mais on s'est bien amusé quand même.

Remember that you can use or adapt any of the above texts for your own Directed Writing piece.

Exercise 58 – You could also try to translate them to practise your translation skills.

What you did in your free time and in the evenings

When talking about what you did during your free time, you should remember where you are supposed to be. As previously mentioned make sure you are aware of what you can do in the area. If you do not know the region or area at all, write about activities that can be done anywhere.

To help you however we will look at different areas in France.

Remember!
Say when you did things and how often, e.g.

When?
le matin/l'après-midi/pendant le temps libres/ pendant la journée/le soir/le week-end, etc.

How often?
tous les jours, de temps en temps, souvent, parfois, etc.

Link your sentences.
ensuite, puis, après avoir, après être, etc.

A Paris

- Comme Paris est une grande ville animée, il y a énormément de choses à faire et à voir.
- On a visité/on a vu/on est allé voir
  - la Tour Eiffel
  - la cathédrale de Notre Dame
  - le Sacré-Cœur
  - les Champs-Elysées
  - le Louvre.
- Nous avons fait des excursions en bateau mouche.
- Une fois on a pris un bateau mouche pour voir Paris de la Seine.
- On a fait de belles promenades le long de la Seine et puis on a visité les monuments historiques.
- On s'est promené dans notre quartier pour voir de beaux bâtiments.
- On a fait du lèche-vitrines, car tout est vraiment cher à Paris.
- Nous avons fait du shopping dans les magasins de luxe de Paris.

Specific vocabulary

- un bateau mouche — *a pleasure boat*
- la Seine — *the river that runs through Paris*

A Grenoble (dans les Alpes)

- Grenoble se trouve dans les Alpes près de la Suisse.
- En hiver c'est une ville très animée, pleine de fanatiques de sports d'hiver.
- En été, il y a beaucoup de touristes qui viennent faire des randonnées en montagne et apprécier de belles vues.
- On s'est bien amusé en faisant
  - du ski
  - de la luge
  - du snow-board
  - du patinage sur le lac
  - des randonnées en montagne
  - de belles promenades autour du lac.
- Il y avait tant de choses à faire. On pouvait
  - faire du ski
  - patiner
  - faire des bonhommes de neige
  - boire du chocolat chaud dans les cafés sur la montagne
  - visiter la vieille ville de Grenoble
  - aller en classe de neige
  - faire de l'alpinisme.
- Une fois on a pris le train pour aller en Suisse où j'ai acheté du bon chocolat pour ma mère.
- Après avoir passé une journée fatigante on sortait au restaurant pour manger les spécialités de cette région.
- Un soir, on a mangé une fondue savoyarde, une vraie spécialité de cette région. C'est une fondue au fromage qu'on mange avec du pain.
- Une fois on a mangé une raclette qui est un plat au fromage fondu qu'on met sur les pommes de terres et du jambon. C'était délicieux.

Specific vocabulary

- après avoir passé — *having spent*
- les randonnées en montagne — *walks in the mountains*
- patiner — *ice-skating*
- les bonhommes de neige — *snowmen*

A Concarneau (en Bretagne)

- Concarneau est une jolie station balnéaire sur la côte Atlantique en Bretagne.
- En été c'est un centre touristique très renommé en France. Par conséquent, il y a un monde fou pendant cette saison.
- On est allé à la plage qui se trouvait à cent mètres seulement de l'hôtel/ de la maison/de l'auberge de jeunesse. C'était génial.
- On a fait des sports aquatiques tels que
  - la planche à voile
  - la voile
  - le surf
  - la plongée sous marine.
- On a joué au volley/au foot/au frisbee sur le sable. On s'est bien amusé.
- On s'est baigné dans la mer qui était un peu froide parfois.
- On a fait des excursions en car pour visiter d'autres villes en Bretagne.
- On a fait des excursions en car pour visiter la côte qui ressemble beaucoup à la côte écossaise.
- On est allé au Mont-St-Michel qui est un joli village avec une très belle église. C'était vraiment beau.
- On est allé au restaurant pour déguster les fruits de mer et le poisson qui sont les spécialités de cette région. C'était vraiment bon.
- Tous les après-midis on allait dans une crêperie pour manger les fameuses crêpes de Bretagne et boire un bol de cidre. C'était super.

Specific vocabulary

- la planche à voile — *windsurfing*
- la plongée sous marine — *under-water diving*
- la côte — *the coast*
- une crêperie — *a pancake restaurant*
- un bol de cidre — *a bowl of cider (speciality of Brittany)*

A Nîmes (en Provence)

- Nîmes est une ville pittoresque et ancienne qui se trouve au nord de la Provence.
- Il y a beaucoup de monuments historiques qui datent de l'époque romaine. C'est vraiment joli comme ville.
- On a fait des excursions en car tout autour de la région pour voir les villes connues comme Avignon, Arles, etc.
- On a visité plein de musées et de monuments historiques.
- On a visité les vignes et on a pu déguster le vin de cette région.
- On a visité la Camargue, une région connue pour ses chevaux blancs et ses taureaux.
- On a fait de l'équitation dans la Camargue sur les chevaux blancs.

Specific vocabulary

- l'époque romaine — *roman times*
- les vignes — *vineyards*
- les taureaux — *bulls*
- faire de l'équitation — *to go horse-riding*

General activities

If you are unsure of the area that you are required to talk about, here are some activities that can be done almost anywhere in France.

Remember to use your dictionary to help with any difficult words.

- On faisait des excursions en car pour visiter d'autres villes dans la région.
- On faisait des excursions en car pour visiter toutes les attractions touristiques de la région.

- On s'est promené dans les rues tout en regardant de beaux magasins.
- Comme on aime bien le sport, on a fait beaucoup de vélo dans les bois non loin de la ville.

- Les jours de soleil, on se bronzait dans le jardin de l'hôtel/de l'auberge de jeunesse/de la maison, etc.
- Les jours de pluie, on visitait les monuments ou on passait du temps à lire.

- On regardait des films vidéos pour améliorer notre français.
- Une fois on est allé au cinéma pour voir un film français. C'était très difficile à comprendre.

Le soir

- On mangeait souvent au restaurant pour déguster de la bonne cuisine française.
- Une fois, j'ai pris des escargots/cuisses de grenouilles en entrée. Je les ai trouvés vraiment bons.
- On mangeait dans de bons restaurants français où on a pu déguster de la cuisine française.
- On sortait en boîte de nuit pour danser et rencontrer les français du coin.
- On allait dans les cafés pour prendre un verre et bavarder sur la terrasse.
- On discutait des événements de la journée.
- On se couchait tôt car on était toujours fatigué après les événements de la journée.

Specific vocabulary

• les bois	– *the woods*
• améliorer	– *to improve*
• déguster	– *to savour/to taste*
• les escargots	– *snails*
• les cuisses de grenouilles	– *frogs legs*
• boîte de nuit	– *night-club*
• bavarder	– *to chat*

> **Remember!**
>
> Be careful with your past tenses.
>
> Imperfect is used for things you did regularly.
>
> Past tense is for a specific past action.

What you thought of the food

As you will no doubt mention the food you had in France, here are a few things you could say.

Try the 'vocabulary timing game' to help you learn the vocabulary.

La nourriture/cuisine française est	– *French food/cuisine is*
• très bonne	– *very good*
• excellente	– *excellent*
• sublime	– *sublime*
• délicieuse	– *delicious*
• meilleure que la cuisine britannique	– *better than British food*
• dégoûtante	– *disgusting*
• trop riche	– *too rich*

> **Remember!**
>
> 'La nourriture' and 'la cuisine' are both feminine so you must make the adjective you use with it agree.

Exercise 59a – Now listen to the three people talking about their time in France.

Take notes on what they did and what they thought of the food.

Check your answers.

If you missed things out, look at the transcript and read it at the same time as listening to the CD to see where you encountered difficulties.

TRACK 41

Were these difficulties due to problems of pronunciation or lack of understanding?

Make a list of the words you did not understand and look them up in the dictionary.

Listen to the CD again to practise the pronunciation of the words you mispronounced.

Exercise 59b – Now try translating these passages into English.

All the vocabulary and expressions from the three passages you have just listened to and read can be used in your Directed Writing.

Now it's your turn.

Write a passage about what you did in an area of France and what the food was like.

Evaluation of the trip

The final bullet point is likely to be your evaluation of the trip. Let's brainstorm some ideas.

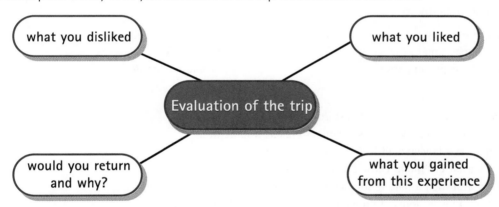

We will now take each idea in turn.

Remember to use your dictionary and that all the phrases and vocabulary can be used in your Directed Writing.

Before looking at specific vocabulary, you should remember the following phrases for concluding and giving your opinions. You will already know a lot of expressions from the pieces of writing you have already done for each of them in the Higher programme, but here is a little reminder.

- toutes choses considerées   – *everything considered*
- ayant pesé le pour et le contre   – *having weighed up the pros and cons*

Followed by:
- je pense que   – *I think that*
- je suis d'avis que   – *I am of the opinion that*
- je crois que   – *I think that*
- je dirais que   – *I would say that*

We are now ready to say what you liked or disliked.

What you liked

Here are some useful expressions that you could use to say what you liked.

- j'ai vraiment aimé ...   – *I really liked ...*
- j'ai adoré ...   – *I loved ...*
- ce qui m'a émerveillé, c'était ...   – *that thing that really amazed me was ...*

Other expressions

- La nourriture était très bonne/sans reproche/délicieuse.
- Le logement était vraiment confortable et bien équipé.
- A mon avis Paris/Grenoble/Nîmes, etc. était ...
  - sensationnel
  - fantastique
  - passionnant
  - joli
  - magnifique
  - beau.
- Il a fait super beau pendant tout le séjour. C'était génial.
- Je me suis très bien amusé(e) pendant ce voyage.
- C'était vraiment une expérience inoubliable.
- C'était un voyage que je n'oublierai jamais.

What you disliked

Here are some useful expressions that you could use to say what you disliked.

- je n'ai pas aimé   – *I didn't like*
- je n'ai pas pu supporter   – *I could not stand*

Other expressions

- La nourriture était affreuse/grasse/trop riche.
- Le logement était sale et les chambres étaient trop petites.
- A mon avis la ville était laide et on s'est vraiment ennuyé.
- Il n'y avait pas grand chose à faire ni à voir.
- Il n'y avait rien à faire le soir, alors on s'ennuyait à mourir après le repas.
- Il a plu tous les jours et on en avait marre de rester dans le car.
- Il n'a pas fait beau alors on n'a pas pu faire tout ce que l'on avait prévu.

Specific vocabulary

- s'ennuyer à mourir   – *to be bored to death*
- en avoir marre   – *to be fed up*
- ce qu'on avait prévu   – *that we had planned*

What did you gain from this experience?

- J'ai beaucoup amélioré mon français.
- C'était très intéressant de découvrir une ville étrangère/un pays étranger/une culture différente.
- Je crois que ce genre de voyage est un bon moyen de
  - rencontrer des gens d'autres cultures
  - apprendre une langue
  - améliorer son français
  - voyager à l'étranger sans trop dépenser
  - voir un autre pays, ses monuments et ses paysages.

Would you return?

The following expressions could be completed by using the ideas you have just seen on what you gained from this experience.

- J'aimerais beaucoup refaire un voyage semblable plus tard parce que …
- J'aimerais bien faire un autre voyage dans un pays étranger car …
- J'espère qu'il y aura d'autres voyages comme celui-là parce que …
- J'aimerais bien retourner en France pour + verb (infintive).

We have now completed all the bullet points.

You will find a couple of scenarios to follow.

Try to write an essay on each scenario, remembering to cover each bullet point fully.

Before you do this however, look at the page on 'common errors' made by pupils when writing in French.

And finally!

Remember – quality is more important than quantity.

Common Errors

1   Be careful that you set the scene according to the instructions and directions that you have been given. Always mention the name of the country – 'en France', even though it may seem obvious to you at this stage.

2   Write in paragraphs.

3   Be very careful with your tenses.

4   Think about what you are writing. Just because you have always used 'accompagnaient' in the plural form does not mean that this is the only form which exists. It may only be one teacher that accompanies you.

5   If you are writing that you stayed somewhere in the past for a certain time, do not use 'pour' but use 'pendant'. For example, 'I worked in France for six weeks' will be 'j'ai travaillé en France pendant six semaines'. Remember that you can use 'pour' for future time but use 'pendant' for past time.

6   If you want to say the train was late, **do not use 'tard'** (which means late at night). You need to use one of the following: '**Le train était en retard**. Le train **avait du retard**. Le train avait un retard **de** deux heures.'

7   If you are talking about food or accommodation and you want to say it was okay, use 'ça allait'.

8   Be careful with 'tout':
    - tout le temps   – *all the time*
    - tous les jours   – *every day*
    - toutes les semaines   – *every week*

9   Remember 'in the evening' = le soir, 'in the afternoon' = l'après-midi, etc.

10 Remember 'a campsite' = un camping; 'a caravan' = une caravane and 'a tent' = une tente.

11 Adjective agreements – think about these carefully. They need to agree in the feminine singular, masculine plural and feminine plural.

12 When you are writing about your job do not use 'un' or 'une' to say what you did, e.g. 'j'ai travaillé comme réceptionniste' not 'j'ai travaillé comme une réceptionniste'.

13 If you are saying what you had to do in your work, you may use 'j'ai dû'. This must be followed by the infinitive of the verb, e.g. 'j'ai dû parler en français'.

14 Be very careful when using 'to' and 'from' in French. To = à, and from = de. Therefore if you want to say 'we took the bus to the campsite' you will have to say 'on a pris l'autobus jusqu'au camping' because campsite is masculine.

15 Similarly 'we departed from Glasgow' would be 'on est parti de Glasgow' – it would however be easier to say 'on a quitté Glasgow'.

16 When you are giving opinions on your stay, use the past tense. 'J'ai beaucoup aimé', or 'j'ai vraiment adoré'. 'J'ai vraiment apprécié l'accueil de mes collègues'.

17 If you want to say 'about' in the context of 'about 15 pupils' use 'environ'. For example, 'environ 15 élèves'. If you are talking about time use 'vers'. For example, 'vers minuit'.

18 Remember that you need to make the past participle agree if you are using reflexive verbs or verbs which take être. If you are a girl you must add an 'e' to the verb. For example, 'je me suis très bien amusée', 'je me suis couchée', etc.

19 I stayed in a hotel = j'ai logé dans un hotel. If you use 'je suis resté dans un hôtel' it means 'I stayed' = remained in a hotel (and did not go out!)

20 Finally always read your essay through at the end to ensure that it makes sense.

Scenario one

Write 150–180 words in French on the following situation.

Your school/college has organised an exchange trip with a French school/college in a small village in the French Alps. You have just spent six weeks there staying with a French family. On your return you have been asked to write an account of your visit for the school magazine in France.

You must include the following information and try to add other relevant details.

- Where you went and for how long.
- Your impressions of the accommodation and town.
- What you liked or disliked about the family.
- What you liked or disliked about the school.
- What you did in your free time.
- Your impressions of the trip and what you gained from this experience.

Scenario two

Write 150–180 words in French on the following situation.

Last summer you went to Paris for one month working and living in a hotel as a waiter(ress). You have now been asked to write a newspaper article in French of your experiences in Paris.

You must include the following information and try to add other relevant details.

- How you got the job and how long you worked for.
- Your impressions of Paris and your accommodation.
- How you got on with your colleagues.
- Details of your job and your duties.
- What you did at the weekends and in the evenings.
- Would you like to do a similar trip and why.

Section 3: Preparation for the External Exam

Speaking: Oral Presentation and Discussion

Paper 1: Reading and Directed Writing

Paper 2: Listening and Writing

SPEAKING Oral Presentation and Discussion

Format of the speaking assessment (25% of marks)

Speaking is assessed in two parts:

1 Oral Presentation – worth 10 marks.

2 Topic Discussion – worth 15 marks.

Both parts of the speaking assessment are recorded on audiocassette and the discussion is conducted with your class teacher. The oral presentation should last for one to two minutes. You will be asked to speak without interruption on a topic that you will have chosen and prepared in advance, and this should allow you to begin the test with confidence starting with a topic with which you are familiar. To help you sustain the presentation, you may have as support five headings of up to eight words each, which will probably be in French but could also be in English.

In the second part of the test, the topic discussion, your teacher will develop a discussion, which begins from the topic that you have presented, but which must also move into other themes and topic areas. Therefore, in this part you will need to listen and respond to the questions which your teacher asks. For example, if you have chosen to begin your presentation with talking about your home life and relationship with your parents (Lifestyles), this might develop into a discussion of whether your plans for the future include staying at home (Education and Work) and whether holidays with or without your parents are more successful (The Wider World). The assessment of the speaking is against criteria, which assess the **content** of your presentation and discussion, the range and variety of the **structures** used and the **grammatical accuracy** of your speaking.

Preparation for the oral presentation

Firstly, remember that you must operate at the level of expressing ideas or opinions, advantages or disadvantages and give some form of conclusion. Therefore, you will need to be aware of ideas and opinions which people hold on each topic and where you stand in relation to them. Having decided on the topic on which you wish to base your presentation, you will need to make use of the help sheets provided in this book, which give you the vocabulary and structures necessary to organise and express your ideas. You will need language **structures** in French, which will help you to present and organise your ideas and arguments. For example in English, phrases like 'firstly', 'secondly', 'in conclusion', 'I would argue that' and 'some might argue that'. **Make sure you can use confidently the phrases provided in this book, which allow you to introduce and link your ideas!** Once you have structured your presentation, you will need to practise presenting it aloud to develop your fluency and confidence.

Having planned your presentation you then need to consider where the discussion may lead and be well prepared to move into other topic areas. **Remember that you have to move into a different theme than the one you started from!** So if your presentation deals with Healthy Living (Lifestyles), the discussion could develop into what facilities/opportunities for leisure activities there are or should be at school (Education and Work) and/or what activities you look for in a holiday (The Wider World). The discussion could continue to cover whether you prefer holidays with or without parents and could end with your general relationship with family/friends, thereby ending with the other main topic in Lifestyles.

Be sure to be prepared for the move from the presentation to the discussion and try to lead the discussion into areas where you are well prepared! Here are some phrases your teacher might use to move you into the discussion. Think about what language you could use from the practice activities in this book.

Possible questions

Something you have said will be picked up and you could be asked:

1 Les rapports familiaux:

• Alors, est-ce que tu t'entends bien avec ta famille en général?

• Est-ce qu'il y a souvent de petites frictions – ou tout se passe sans conflit dans ta famille?

- Chez moi, il y a souvent des disputes quand la télé est allumée ou quand il y a des tâches ménagères à faire. Qu'est-ce qui provoque des disputes chez toi?

2   Vivre en ville ou à la campagne?

- Evidemment tu fais beaucoup de choses intéressantes pendant ton temps libre/pour garder la forme et te maintenir en bonne santé. Si on vit à la campagne on n'a pas un si grand choix de distractions, mais il y a d'autres avantages. Qu'est-ce que tu préfères en fin de compte – vivre en ville ou … ?

- Tu m'as parlé de la pollution qu'il y a dans les grandes villes. Et je suis d'accord – moi, je déteste la pollution provoquée par les gazs d'échappements et je n'aime pas du tout le bruit incessant de la ville. Est-ce que c'est important pour toi – d'être en bonne santé et de vivre dans un environnement plutôt sain?

- Peut-être préférerais-tu vivre dans un petit village?

- Quels sont les avantages d'une grande ville pour un étudiant?

3   La télévision

- Evidemment tu penses qu'il est important de te maintenir en bonne santé. Tu fais des efforts pour garder la forme – mais c'est difficile quelquefois. Quand tu ne fais pas du sport qu'est-ce que tu fais pendant tes moments de loisirs?

- Quels sont les aspects positifs de la télé, à ton avis?

- Quels sont les aspects negatifs/les dangers de … ?

- Est-ce que tu regardes trop la télé, à ton avis?

4   La bonne santé

- Est-ce important pour toi de te maintenir en bonne santé?

- Tu m'as dit que tu regardes trop la télé et rester assis tout le temps n'est vraiment pas bon pour la santé. Est-ce que tu penses que tu as une vie assez saine ou pas?

- Si tu regardes la télé trois heures par jour, quand est-ce que tu as le temps de faire tes devoirs?

Leading to school …

- Parlons maintenant de l'école. Dis-moi ce que tu penses du lycée en général. Qu'est-ce qu'un bon lycée, par exemple?

- Est-ce que tu es dans un bon lycée, à ton avis?

- Si tu sors beaucoup, tu regardes la télé et tu fais certains travaux ménagers… quand est-ce que tu fais tes devoirs?

- Est-ce que tu as beaucoup de devoirs à faire cette année?

- Qu'est-ce que tu étudies comme matières cette année?

- Est-ce qu'il est important d'avoir de bons profs dans un lycée, à ton avis?

- Je vois que tu ne portes pas d'uniforme scolaire. Est-ce que tu penses que l'uniforme est important dans une école?

- Tu m'as parlé de ta vie à Glasgow? Est-ce que tu vas rester à Glasgow après le lycée, ou est-ce que tu voudrais partir ailleurs?

- Quels sont tes projets pour l'avenir?

So, in preparation for the presentation and discussion, you will need to consider:

1   the selection of the topic for presentation

2   the content and structure of the presentation

3   the five headings which you can bring as support

4   practising doing the presentation

5 improving pronunciation and intonation

6 developing links to continue into the topic discussion.

Although this is a test of speaking, a lot of your preparation will involve writing and refining what you intend to say.

Assessment of Speaking

Your performance in both parts of the speaking assessment is assessed by your teacher against the following 'pegged-mark descriptors'.

Categories	Criteria	Pegged marks	
		Presentation	Discussion/Interact
Very Good	Confident handling of language with a high level of accuracy. Speaks fluently and without undue hesitation, or where there is some hesitation recovers well, and generally goes beyond minimal responses. Wide range of vocabulary and structures appropriate to Higher level. Immediate and almost total understanding of almost everything said. Pronunciation and intonation sufficient to be readily understood by a speaker of the language.	10	15
Good	The language is mostly accurate, with a wide range of vocabulary and structures appropriate to this level. Speaks fluently and without undue hesitation, or where there is some hesitation recovers well, and readily goes beyond minimal responses. Understands almost everything said. Pronunciation and intonation sufficient to be generally understood by a speaker of the language.	8	12
Satisfactory	Completes task, demonstrating sufficient accuracy in a range of vocabulary and structures appropriate to this level, to convey meaning clearly, in spite of errors. May be hesitant and give only minimal correct responses or speak at greater length with less accuracy. Capable of coming to an understanding of all that is said. Pronunciation and intonation sufficient to be understood by a sympathetic speaker of the language.	6	9
Unsatisfactory (Near Miss)	Difficulty in achieving communication because of limited range of vocabulary and structures and/or serious inaccuracies in language appropriate to Higher level. Understands most of what is said clearly and slowly by a sympathetic speaker. May speak with a considerable degree of hesitation, but makes some attempt to recover. Pronunciation and intonation sufficient to be generally understood by a sympathetic speaker of the language.	4	6
Poor	Communication seriously impeded by inadequate vocabulary and structures and/or by gross errors in language appropriate to Higher level. Frequently has difficulty in understanding what is said, even with help. There may be occasional other tongue interference. Pronunciation and intonation may be such as to require clarification, even from a sympathetic speaker of the language.	2	3
Very Poor	No redeeming features.	0	0

This type of marking is often referred to as 'impression marking' as the marker is trying to form an impression of which category most accurately describes your performance. You should also look on it as your chance to 'impress' the marker so that you achieve the highest mark of which you are capable, therefore it is important to know what is likely to influence the marker.

Each category from Very Good to Very Poor contains the following three elements in its descriptors:

Content or structure – this means you will need to use the phrases suggested for organising your presentation and you will need to ensure that you develop each topic at a level appropriate to Higher, as indicated in the introduction to each topic development strand.

Grammatical accuracy or ease of comprehension – this evaluates how well a French native speaker would understand what you are saying. This will partly depend on your accent and how well you pronounce the words in French, so make use of the recordings provided to make sure you sound as much like the person on the recording as possible. This will also depend on how accurately you speak and in particular how clear it is which verb tense you are using. If the person is unclear as to whether you are talking about the past, the present or the future, then comprehension is likely to be in doubt. Therefore, it is essential that you can handle the present, past and future forms of the essential verbs accurately.

Range and variety of vocabulary and language structures – even if you use only a limited range of vocabulary and structures you should achieve the Satisfactory category as long as the content is appropriate and the accuracy is enough to ensure comprehension. However, to achieve the Good and Very Good categories, you need to try and use more adventurous and more demanding language structures (this is the type of language we have concentrated on throughout this book). If you have a variety of ways of introducing ideas and of linking sentences, if you can use the sort of phrases used naturally by the native speakers on the recordings and if you can maintain a high level of accuracy, you will have done enough to gain the Very Good mark. If you try all of this but make quite a few errors in doing so, it is likely you will get the Good mark as being 'enterprising but less accurate'.

Given that you choose, prepare and practise the presentation in advance and given that the discussion must remain within the prescribed themes, it should be possible to be well prepared and able to give your best performance. Certainly if you select from the language used in this book and practise using it in the ways suggested until it becomes your own and you can use it with confidence, you should have a very good mark in the bank before you move on to the written examination.

PAPER 1 Reading and Directed Writing

Format of the assessment

This paper lasts 1 hour and 40 minutes and is divided into two sections: Section 1 – Reading and Translation and Section 2 – Directed Writing. There is no official break between the sections, therefore you will have to decide yourself when you move on to Section 2. As a guide, the notional amount of time is approximately 1 hour for the Reading and Translation and 40 minutes for the Directed Writing.

Section 1: Reading and Translation (20 + 10 = 30%)

The Reading passage is usually about 650 words in length and the content of the passage is usually drawn from a magazine article and related to the prescribed themes of Lifestyles, Education and Work and The Wider World. The passage is used to test reading comprehension and the underlined section of the text is used to test the ability to translate accurately from French into English. **It is important that you are aware of the difference between the skills involved in comprehension and translation.**

Preparation and exam technique

Always begin with the Reading Comprehension questions, which are worth 20 of the 30 marks available. The introduction in English sets the context of the passage and if you read the questions in English quickly, you will get further indication of what happens in the passage and how it breaks into different sections and sub-topics. Now read through the text to see how much you can understand, remembering that some unusual words may be given in the glossary at the end of the text. Such words will be numbered in the text. You do have the use of a dictionary but use it sparingly as you will not have time to look up lots of words. If you have built up your vocabulary (by using the techniques indicated earlier) and if you use your knowledge of English and French, you should be able to understand the text with only the occasional use of the dictionary.

For example in the 2002 Paper, you know from the introduction and questions that the text is about someone who changes his lifestyle dramatically and who organises something called the 'Sénégazelle', which allows him to save lives in Dakar. You should recognise the vocabulary related to 'Lifestyles' and can use your knowledge of the context of the story and knowledge of English and French to read the text fairly quickly. A lot of the words look like English words and (apart from a few 'false friends') they usually mean the same, e.g. 'sponsorisées' = sponsored. Sometimes it is the context that helps you work out the meaning, e.g. 'pour aider les enfants à l'orphelinat de Dakar'. Here the difficult word is 'l'orphelinat' but if you understand the rest of the sentence, it is fairly obvious that it means orphanage, which you might also have worked out from your knowledge of English. Later in the text you find the word 'les orphelins', which you can see from your knowledge of French is a plural noun 'the ...' and must surely be the orphans. **There will be words you want to check in the dictionary but only use it if the other techniques fail**.

1 Read the text for understanding and demonstrate that understanding by answering the questions in clear and comprehensible English.

2 Take each question in turn as the questions follow logically through the text, with question one dealing with the opening paragraph and so on. The question will usually guide you to specific lines in the text, so read these lines carefully.

3 Look at the number of points available for the question carefully, e.g. three points usually require three pieces of information.

4 Then answer the question in as much detail as you can. You must answer the question in clear English and not rely on the marker to work out what you might have meant. **Remember you do NOT have to translate all of the lines indicated**. In the 2002 Paper, candidates were asked to describe how a plane accident happened and would find the answer in this passage: 'Un jour, j'ai eu une panne de moteur, je suis passé entre deux lignes de haute tension, et j'ai atterri en catastrophe'. A perfect answer would be something like: I had engine failure (the engine or motor broke down), I passed between two power lines (electricity cables/high tension cables) and had to make an emergency landing. The markers are not looking for any one particular wording but they are looking for proof that you have understood what has happened. If you simply give a word for word translation you are likely to lose marks by leaving the marker in doubt as to whether you really understand how these individual words make sense in this passage. For example, someone who answered: 'I passed by two lines of high tension and landed in catastrophe' is unlikely to score any points for this question. **So make sure that it is not awkward use of English rather than lack of comprehension of the French that costs you marks**.

Markers are also instructed not to give credit for information that may be correct but that is surrounded by so much that is wrong or incomprehensible as to leave the marker in doubt as to whether comprehension has taken place. So it is very important that you read over your answer and make sure it makes sense to you and says what you want it to mean! Markers are also instructed not to transfer information for candidates from question to question. For example, if you give as your answer to question three, information that would have been the correct answer for question four, the marker will mark it wrong for question three and will mark question four separately. The marker will not move your correct information for you. **So, again, it is important that you answer exactly what each question asks!**

Translation into English

The last question requires you to translate accurately a section of the text, which is underlined. It is important that you attempt the translation section after having done the reading comprehension questions. By this time you will know what the text is about and will now be asked to look carefully at an important part of the text and translate accurately what it means.

The translation into English is allocated 10 marks. The section for translation is divided into a number of sub-sections or sense units (normally 5). Each sense unit is worth 2 marks, which are awarded according to the quality and accuracy of the translation into English. The descriptions detailed on the following page are used to assess the candidate's performance. Each sense unit is awarded one of the marks shown.

Category	Mark	Description
Good	2	Essential information and relevant details are understood and conveyed clearly and accurately, with appropriate use of English.
Satisfactory	1	Essential information is understood and conveyed clearly and comprehensibly, although some of the details may be translated in an imprecise or inaccurate manner. The key message is conveyed in spite of inaccuracies and weaknesses in the use of English.
Unsatisfactory	0	The candidate fails to demonstrate sufficient understanding of the essential information and relevant details. Errors may include mistranslation and/or the failure to translate relevant details.

This means that if you translate all that is there accurately, and in suitable English, you will score 2 marks; if you translate everything but are inaccurate or use awkward English you will still score 1 mark and if you fail to translate a word or make a serious error you will fail to score any marks for that sense unit. In this task the markers are looking for accuracy and clear English rather than imaginative translation, so it is best to stick fairly closely to the same sequence and structures as the French sense units. You will not have much difficulty in finding the meaning of each French word but in order to translate accurately, you will also need to be careful and make accurate use of your knowledge of French grammar, to show how the words are related to each other.

The most common errors often result from carelessness and this can cost a lot of marks. In particular, you must make sure you have translated all of each sense unit. Pay particular attention to the words that come in front of the nouns and be sure to translate them accurately:

- un/une/des   – *a/some*
- le/la/les   – *the*
- ce/cette/ces   – *this/these; that/those*
- mon/ma/mes   – *my*
- ton/ta/tes   – *your*
- son/sa/ses   – *his/her*
- notre/nos   – *our*
- votre/vos   – *your*
- leur/leurs   – *their*

The verbs are another area where candidates often lose marks by not identifying the appropriate tense. Most recognise the present and perfect tense but forget that in English you have a choice of how to translate them:

- Je joue   – *I play/am playing/do play.*
- J'ai joué   – *I played/have played/did play.*
- Je vais   – *I go/am going/do go.*
- Je suis allé   – *I went/have gone/did go.*

Remember you have the choice and be sure to select the one that best fits the passage. Again, be careful that you don't lose marks because of inappropriate use of English.

The other tenses can be harder to recognise and therefore to translate. The future (will) and the conditional (would) share the same stem, the conditional (would) and the imperfect (was ___ing/used to) share the same endings and the pluperfect (had) contains the imperfect of avoir/être and has the same past participle as the perfect (have)! Are you sure which is which and what the equivalents are in English?

- J'attendais le bus   – *I was waiting for the bus/used to wait for the bus.*
- J'attendrais le bus   – *I would wait for the bus.*
- J'attendrai le bus   – *I will wait for the bus.*
- J'ai attendu le bus   – *I waited for the bus/have waited for the bus.*
- J'avais attendu le bus   – *I had waited for the bus.*

One construction to look out for is **'depuis'** and the effect it has on the tense of the verb. The only tenses used with this construction in French are the present and the imperfect but look how they are translated in English:

- J'attends le bus
- J'attends le bus depuis vingt minutes

- J'habite en Ecosse
- J'habite en Ecosse depuis trois ans
- J'attendais le bus
- J'attendais le bus depuis vingt minutes
- J'habitais en Ecosse
- J'habitais en Ecosse depuis trois ans

– *I am waiting for the bus.*
– *I have been waiting for the bus for twenty minutes.*

– *I live in Scotland.*
– *I have been living in Scotland for three years.*
– *I was waiting for the bus.*
– *I had been waiting for the bus for twenty minutes.*
– *I was living in Scotland.*
– *I had been living in Scotland for three years.*

If you are careful, revise your grammar and check your English, you can score full marks in this task. It is to get you into this good habit that the book contains so many activities where you are encouraged to translate accurately what you read or hear.

Section 2: Directed Writing (15% of marks)

This task requires you to write at least 150 words in French. You are given a scenario in English, usually involving you and a group in a visit to France. You are required to write an account of the visit and are given information in English that you must include in your French report. This information in English is given in the form of six bullet points.

Addressing the bullet points

The task is intended to be fairly predictable and therefore the bullet points tend to follow an established pattern.

Points 1 and 2 are entirely predictable and let you set the scene by giving details as to where you went, how you travelled, where you stayed, how many were in the group and what the journey/accommodation was like.

Points 3 and 4 tend to focus on the purpose of the visit and ask what you did and what you thought of it or of the people you met.

Points 5 and 6 are less predictable but tend to ask you to give your reaction to the visit, e.g. what was best/worst about it and what benefit you gained from the trip, or how you will continue contact after the visit.

You must address all bullet points but are free to develop some points more fully than others. If a bullet point contains two elements, e.g. how you travelled **and** where you stayed, then you must address **both** elements. To achieve the top 'Very Good' mark, you are expected to address the topic 'fully' and in 'a clear and structured manner'. Therefore, if you produce a very unbalanced essay by covering 3 or 4 of the more predictable bullet points in detail and writing very little on the other 2/3 bullets, it is unlikely that you will be awarded the 'Very Good' mark.

The Assessment Process and Exam Technique

Writing in French is assessed in a very similar way to that described in the assessment of Speaking. The marker reads all that you have written (even if it is well over the suggested maximum of 180 words) and assesses the overall quality of your answer against the pegged-mark categories and criteria. Again it is 'impression marking' and the marker will allocate the most appropriate mark to your written work. The marker then checks that all 6 bullet points have been addressed and, if they have, he confirms the impression mark. If a bullet point has not been addressed, the marker deducts 2 marks and does the same for each bullet point not addressed, up to a maximum of 3 bullets. If 3 or more bullet points have not been addressed the performance will be awarded 0, irrespective of the quality of the language. **So it is very important that you are well prepared to write something for each bullet point**.

The practice material in the Directed Writing section of this book will leave you very well prepared for whatever scenario and bullet points are set in the exam. The Directed Writing task is designed to allow you to reuse language that you have practised and can use confidently, so there is no need to invent new language on the day. Your aim should be to reuse material that you have learned and know is correct, while adapting it to fit the specific bullet points set in the task. Try to 'impress' the marker by showing the range of your vocabulary, structures and grammatical knowledge and by your ability to link short sentences into longer, more complex ones. **Above all, resist the temptation to write an account in English, which you then try to turn into French with the aid of the dictionary**. This is certain to lead to an '**Unsatisfactory**', '**Poor**' or even '**Very Poor**' performance because some parts will be '**incomprehensible to a native speaker**' and will contain bad examples of '**mother tongue interference**' (thinking in English not in French!)

For further information on how writing is assessed and to see the table used to award the marks for writing at Higher Level, see page 87.

PAPER 2 ▶ Listening and Writing (20 + 10 = 30% of marks)

Format of the assessment

This paper lasts 1 hour and is divided into two sections: Section 1 – Listening Comprehension and Section 2 – Writing. The amount of time allocated to each task is normally 20 minutes for Listening and 40 minutes for Writing and you move onto the Writing task once you have completed your answers to the Listening.

Section 1: Listening

You will listen to a conversation between two native speakers of French, usually one male and one female. They will be discussing topics taken from the prescribed themes, which will be very similar to the topics contained in this book and very similar to the topics which you will have prepared for the Speaking assessment. Although there are two speakers, there will be one main speaker with the second speaker normally asking questions and steering the discussion. The questions are in English and require you to give 20 points of information (20 marks) all of which will come from what is said by the main speaker. You will hear the recording twice with a pause of 2 minutes between playings and you can make notes at any time.

Preparation and exam technique

Before you hear the recording you will have time to look at the introduction and questions in English. It is really important that you do this! The introduction in English will set the context of the passage and if you read the questions in English quickly, you will get further indication of what happens in the passage and how the passage breaks into different sections and sub-topics. Look carefully at the questions and study what sort of information is required for each one and how much information is required – again the number of marks allocated to each question will guide you. From the context and the questions try to anticipate the French you might expect to hear, e.g.

- Where?   – prepositions: in/on/near etc. (en/dans/sur/près de etc.)
  and places: in town/Paris/Scotland etc. (en ville/à Paris/en Ecosse etc.)
- When?   – time phrases: last summer/next June etc. (l'été dernier/en Juin prochain etc.)
- How?   – adverbs: quietly/by plane etc. (sans bruit/par avion etc.)
- What ... like? – adjectives: friendly/tiring etc. (sympa/fatigante etc.)
- Why?   – reasons: because/in order to etc. (parce que/pour etc.)

When the recording is playing, **it is important to use your time to listen rather than write**. You may want to write down in French some words you have heard so that you can check them in the dictionary, but keep any notes very short so that you do not lose track of what is being said on the recording. In the two minutes between recordings, study the questions again in detail, remember where the answers came on the recording and note any points that you think you already have. During the final playing, try to confirm the points you thought you had and try to get any details that you had missed during the first playing. When the recording has finished, write up your final answers, making sure that you score out any notes that you do not wish to be marked. Don't leave alternative answers, because unless both of them are correct and were on the recording, you will lose the point.

As with the assessment of Reading, the markers are instructed not to transfer information for candidates from question to question, **so you must give the correct information for the appropriate question**. The markers are also instructed not to give credit for information that may be correct but that is surrounded by a lot that is wrong and was not included on the recording, so there is no benefit and potentially a lot of damage to be done in including information that you did not in fact hear. This is most often seen in response to a question such as: What did she study at university? (2 points) Correct answer: chemistry and computing. Candidate's answer: chemistry, physics, maths and engineering. This candidate would not score any marks although chemistry is correct because of the amount of wrong information that was not included on the recording.

So beware of guessing and listing information in the hope that some of it will be correct!

Better to be well prepared! However, Listening in French is not easy and words which you would recognise if you were reading them can be hard to pick up when you hear them. **That is why this book has concentrated so much on providing you with recordings of the sort of language you can expect to hear in the exam and why it has encouraged you to practise your own pronunciation.** If you know the correct pronunciation of words then you are better placed to picture what is said on the recording. If you have worked through the activities in this book and have made good use of the recordings, you will be well placed to understand the topics and issues that are likely to feature in this part of the exam.

However, it is also worth doing some targeted revision of key words that are likely to appear and which will affect how accurately you answer the questions (the exercises in this book on 'negatives' is a good starting point). It is surprising the number of 'easy' marks that are lost through not recognising **numbers** as they appear in times and prices and through not knowing accurately **days**, **months**, **seasons** and **weather** expressions. Another reason why marks are often lost is that answers are not sufficiently detailed or accurate. This is most often seen in answer to Where? questions. The candidate often understands the place but forgets to concentrate on the preposition. For example, in the 2002 Paper, one question asked: Where did she stay during term time? The answer was 'pas loin de la faculté' = not far from/near the university. Lots of answers gave 'in the university/on the university campus' which is not the same as 'pas loin de'. So it is well worth spending some time revising French prepositions including: **à côté de/près de/en face de** as well as the more common **sur/sous**, etc. **Also remember to practise the correct pronunciation of these words and all vocabulary, because the more accurately you pronounce words the more easily you will recognise them when others pronounce them!**

Section 2: Writing

The Writing task is related to the topic of the Listening and requires you to write a personal response to the issues discussed by the native speakers. You are given a stimulus in French, which indicates how you should structure your response and your response should be between 120–150 words in length. Again the good news is that you should be very familiar with the topics on which you have to write, as they will be very similar to the topics you will have developed in preparation for the Speaking assessment. Through the course of the year with your teacher and through the activities in this book, you will have prepared pieces of writing on all of the topic development strands that are likely to appear in the writing stimulus. The task on the day of the exam should be to **select**, **adapt** and **structure** pieces of writing that you have practised and can use with confidence and which best address the topic set in the stimulus. **You should not expect to simply regurgitate a whole pre-learned essay but should still have learned material that you can use and recombine to produce a relevant and accurate essay.**

Let's look at the 2002 Paper as an example! The stimulus was: **'Adèle était contente d'aller à Montpellier après avoir quitté l'école. Et vous, avez-vous un endroit préféré où vous aimeriez habiter? Comptez-vous rester chez vous ou aller vivre ailleurs? Pour quelles raisons? Ecrivez 120-150 mots en français pour exprimer vos idées.'** It is important to read the stimulus carefully to be sure you know what is being asked. A candidate who sees only 'après avoir quitté l'école' and writes a prepared essay on leisure activities 'after school' or on 'my future career' will be marked 0 as the essay is irrelevant to the questions set.

If planning to write this essay, it would be useful to brainstorm the sort of things you know, have prepared and can use (remember the spider diagrams in the book!):

Un endroit préféré?	Description of home area – advantages/disadvantages
	Living in town or country – advantages/disadvantages
	Ideal (holiday) destination
Rester chez soi?	Relationship with parents
	Causes of friction in the family
	Future career > university > living with parents or sharing with friends

This plan would show you that you have a lot of material to reuse. Now you need to select and structure your best response. It is important to prepare good beginnings to link the paragraphs and to build up to an effective ending. This is similar to what you did in preparing for the Oral Presentation and many of the phrases you used then can now be used in written form. Once you have written your essay, be sure to check it over to ensure it is as accurate as possible. **As this is a written exam spelling, genders and endings are now very important, so be sure to use your knowledge of grammar to check that subjects and verbs match up!**

Assessment

'Impression marking' is also used to assess this piece of writing and indeed the same pegged-mark descriptors and categories are used here as were used in assessing the Directed Writing task. The marker again reads all that you have written, even if it greatly exceeds the upper limit of 150 words. Try to be selective and structure what you write (you will easily have enough). If you go on too far beyond the limit, you may find that the good impression you were building is undone by errors creeping in as you get tired or careless and you may end up with a lower category than you would have been given, if you had stopped earlier.

Here is the table that is used to award the mark for the writing task.

Category	Criteria	Paper I	Paper II
Very Good	The language is mostly accurate. Can form complex sentences, including a range of structure and vocabulary, and makes appropriate use of learned material. Content addresses the topic fully, and is presented in a clear and structured manner.	15	10
Good	The language is clearly comprehensible throughout, and fairly free of serious errors. Contains a reasonable range of vocabulary and structures. Content is fairly predictable but is mostly relevant and has an adequate sense of structure.	12	8
Satisfactory	The language is sufficiently accurate to convey meaning clearly. Errors may be quite frequent but will not be serious. Can handle tenses, but relies on a limited range of vocabulary and structures. There may be some awkward use of memorised material. Content is free of serious irrelevancies and has some sense of structure.	9	6
Unsatisfactory	The language is insufficiently accurate to convey meaning clearly and consistently. Very limited range of vocabulary and structures. Inappropriate use of learned material, and possibly some unidiomatic translation from English. Content may be partially irrelevant (Essay) and lacking in structure.	6	4
Poor	The language contains frequent basic errors and/or other tongue interference which seriously impede communication. Content may be seriously deficient and unstructured or (Essay) partly irrelevant.	3	2
Very Poor	Largely incomprehensible to a native speaker. No redeeming feature or (Essay) totally irrelevant.	0	0

It is important that you know the key features of the different categories that will be used in assessing your writing. Let's start with 'Satisfactory' to see what is required to ensure we pass at least! The first two descriptors are very important in establishing the level but must be taken together – 'The language is **sufficiently accurate** to convey meaning **clearly**. Errors may be **frequent** but are **not** generally of a serious nature.' The ability to form the necessary verb tenses is crucial in determining whether communication is achieved. A satisfactory performance normally contains a limited number of common verbs and although some of the verbs may contain an error, e.g. j'ai resté, you are in no doubt as to the meaning and tense being used. If the candidate can handle a limited range of common verbs with sufficient accuracy, then it is likely that communication will be achieved in spite of errors in other areas such as spelling, cases, genders and agreements. The other serious error, which can prevent a performance remaining as 'Satisfactory' is the appearance of 'mother tongue interference', usually caused by the candidate 'thinking in English' or misusing the dictionary. In the 'Unsatisfactory' category, errors become more frequent and more of them are of a serious nature (verbs and mother tongue interference). The verb errors become more pronounced and impede clear communication because the reader is left in doubt as to the meaning and tense being used, e.g. no part of avoir/être/no past participle/part of avoir/être + infinitive. It is in this category that mother tongue interference often becomes a feature and contributes to the language becoming 'insufficiently accurate to convey meaning **clearly and consistently**'. By the time we are considering the 'Very Poor' category, the language structure has crumbled and you are looking for a few correct words or phrases. These correct parts are submerged in so much that would be incomprehensible to a native speaker, that no credit can be given, as the task set would not have been accomplished.

Now you know what you need to avoid doing, let's see what will get you the top marks! If we move upwards from the 'Satisfactory' category, we look for a higher level of accuracy and a wider range of vocabulary and structures. In the 'Good' category, performances tend to contain vocabulary and structures which are less basic and therefore the content is becoming more interesting. The language is '**fairly free of serious errors**', which means there may still be errors in spelling, genders, agreements, etc. and there may still be occasional errors in verb tenses, but these will be of the 'j'ai allé' type, which leave you in no doubt as to the tense and meaning. Errors tend to occur when the candidate tries to use more complex language (less common verbs/wider range of structures) and tries to form longer, more complex sentences. Performances in this category are often described as being either 'more accurate but predictable and pedestrian' or 'less accurate but more enterprising and fluent'. If the candidate was able to combine both the accuracy and the wider range of structures, then the performance would move into the 'Very Good' category. In the 'Very Good' category, the language should be '**mostly accurate**'. Therefore, while some errors will still occur, they will be relatively minor and the overall impression is of the ability to sustain a high level of accuracy in verb tenses and to extend this accuracy into other areas of language such as genders, cases, word order and agreements. The candidate attempts to form longer and more complex sentences regularly and tries to introduce less common verbs, vocabulary and language structures, which might include some of the following: reflexive verbs, verbs followed by à/de + infinitive and après avoir/être construction.

If you have practised the activities in this book and have learned the key language for the topic development strands, then this exam will allow you to show what you are capable of and will reward you for the hard work you have done.

Section 4: Test Yourself: Final Revision

Yes, you have now come to the end of the book and probably your Higher Year, but don't start celebrating quite yet.

To help with your revision for the exam, we have made up some sentences for you to translate into French on each theme.

Remember to think about the grammatical structures and the spellings of words.

You can check your answers on pages 28 – 31 of the answer section.

Lifestyles and The Wider World

Family

I am going to give you my opinions on my family relationships.

I get on well with my family.

I have to share a room with my sister and I don't like that.

Of course there are often small arguments at home about ...

We often argue about the housework, my homework, etc.

I hate tidying my room. It's always untidy and my parents tell me off (about it).

I like living at home.

I have had a very good upbringing and have a good relationship with my parents.

I feel at home.

I would bring my children up the same way.

It is important to be independent.

I would like to have my own flat so I could do what I wanted.

I would like to move away as I get on better with my family at a distance.

I wouldn't want to leave home because I would have to do all the housework myself.

I would miss my family and friends if I moved away.

Ideal parents are – understanding, friendly, strict but fair, funny, helpful and caring.

Friendship

In my opinion, friendship is very important.

I trust my friends and family.

A good friend is trustworthy, fun and friendly.

My best friends are called ...

We have the same tastes and interests.

I could not cope without my friends.

A good friend is always there for you.

What I can't stand in a friend is jealousy.

Holidays with or without Parents?

I prefer to go on holiday with my parents as they pay for everything.

I prefer to go on holiday with my friends rather than my family.

There are of course advantages and disadvantages in going on holiday with your parents/friends.

Every year since I was young, I have spent my holidays with my parents.

I love going away with my parents because they have a very young mentality.

They give me money when I need it.

I would prefer to go on holiday with my friends. You can do what you like, when you like.

I would prefer to go on holiday with my friends, but my parents think I am too young to cope.

Ideal Holidays/Tourism

My ideal holiday would be on an island in the sun because I love the sea and hot weather.

My ideal holiday would be in Iceland because it is very interesting and there would be many things to see and do.

Scotland is a beautiful country, full of tradition.

It does rain a lot in Scotland but the scenery is beautiful.

Tourism is very important to Scotland.

Home Area

I love living in town because there is a lot to do (there).

Everything is close by.

The city is always lively and the nightlife is excellent.

There are many advantages and disadvantages of living in town/in the country/by the sea.

In the city there are a lot of people and cars and therefore a lot of pollution.

There is also a lot of noise in the city.

The city is polluted by exhaust fumes from the cars.

I would hate to live in town/in the country/by the sea.

If I lived in the country, I would be bored to death.

I would prefer to live in the city/by the sea/in the country because ...

The air is fresh and clean in the country.

If you live in the country you can go for lots of beautiful walks.

I would like to live abroad and learn about different cultures.

Leisure and Healthy Living

A healthy lifestyle is very important to me.

I eat very healthily and do a lot of sport to keep fit.

To stay healthy you should have a balanced diet and do some exercise.

You should not smoke as this can cause cancer and other serious illnesses.

Smoking also makes your skin grey.

You should only drink alcohol in moderation.

You should drink a lot of water.

Unfortunately many young people eat, smoke and drink too much.

Many young people also drink and drive which is extremely dangerous.

Television and Films

I love watching TV and going to the cinema.

My favourite TV programmes are soaps and documentaries.

TV can be a good thing as you can learn a lot about different countries.

In my opinion TV can be very dangerous as there are too many violent programs and too much advertising on TV.

I prefer going to the cinema as I like watching films on the big screen.

Watching French films helps to improve my French.

Education and Work

School and Teachers

A good school should have good teachers.

A good school is one where exam results are good, pupils feel safe and there is a good atmosphere.

A good teacher is – fair, understanding, patient, tolerant, funny, helpful, has a good sense of humour and doesn't give too much homework.

On the other hand, a bad teacher is – always in a bad mood, unfair and doesn't explain clearly.

In my school we have to wear uniform.

Having said that many pupils do not wear the uniform.

In my opinion older pupils should not have to wear uniform.

This year at school, I am studying five subjects at Higher Level.

I love sport and am a member of the hockey club at school.

There are some very good clubs in our school.

Future Aspirations

Next year I am going to stay at school/go to university/take a gap year/find a job.

When I leave school, I would like to go to university and study (there).

I would also like to go to France, to improve my French and learn more about French people and their culture.

I would like to live in France because I hear that the people are very friendly there and the food is delicious.

Career and Unemployment

I would like to be a teacher because I like working with children.

I want to go to work in France because I want to get to know another culture.

I want to be able to communicate well with French people.

Unemployment is a problem everywhere, mainly because of new technology and computers which have replaced man.

Computers are a good thing because they are quick and reduce the amount of paper.

Section 5: Glossary

Glossary of Grammar Terms

Throughout the book grammar terms are used.

You should know all of these but here is a quick glossary to explain what they are in case you have forgotten.

Verbs/Tenses

Infinitive	– the infinitive of a verb is the whole verb – e.g. to do, to say, to go, etc. In French the infinitive ends in 'er', 're' or 'ir'.
The stem	– to form the stem of the verb in French, simply remove the 'er', 'ir', or 're' ending.
Present tense	– this is a tense which is happening now, or an everyday event – e.g. I am going home, I go home at 4pm. In French there is only one form of the present tense.
Perfect tense	– this is a tense describing an action in the past or one that has finished, e.g. I did, I have done.
Imperfect tense	– this is an action which was on-going in the past, e.g. I was doing.
Future	– these are actions which will or can happen.
Conditional tense	– this is an action that would or could happen.
Pronouns	– words such as 'I, you, he, she' are personal pronouns.

Answer Section

This section includes:

- answers to all the activities contained in the main text

- versions in English of the key sentences which you were encouraged to translate from French.

Lifestyles and The Wider Worlc

Exercise 1 – translation (see page 12 and transcript 1)

I trust my older sister.

I get on well with my parents.

I feel close to my younger brother.

I always confide in my best friend.

Exercise 2a – listening (see page 13 and transcript 2)

J'ai une sœur et un frère mais je fais plus confiance à mon frère aîné car je sais qu'il peut garder un secret.

Je fais partie d'une famille nombreuse et je m'entends très bien avec tout le monde.

Je suis fille unique et donc je me sens très proche de mes parents.

Je me confie toujours à ma sœur jumelle car on est très proche l'une de l'autre.

(Remember your accents and, although not pronounced, do not forget the 's' at the end of words such as parents, très, sens, etc.)

Exercise 2b – translation (see page 13 and transcript 2)

I have a sister and a brother but I trust my older brother more because I know he can keep a secret.

I have a large family/I am part of a large family and get on very well with everyone/everybody.

I am an only child (daughter) and I am therefore very close to my parents.

I always confide in my twin sister because we are very close to each other.

Exercise 3 – Test Yourself (see pages 14 to 15)

1 b – it should read: Je ne me sens pas proche de mon frère.

2 b – the others should read: Ma sœur ne fait rien à la maison,

Je n'ai rien senti.

Il n'a rien dit.

3 c

4 a and d – the others should read: Il ne fait jamais confiance à sa belle-mère.

Ma sœur n'est jamais énervante.

5 d

6 d

7 c – you do not use 'pas' with 'ne ... ni ... ni'

8 d – it should read: Mes amis ne me font plus confiance.

Family Conflicts – Les Conflits Familiaux

Exercise 4 – translation (see page 16)

There are often arguments because of housework.

There are often arguments because of money.

My parents and I often argue about my boy/girl friend.

My mother always tells me off if I don't do my homework.

My parents criticise me/reproach me for being too cheeky.

There are often things that create tensions within the family.

What annoys me about my parents is that they want to know everything about my private life.

I always need to ask for permission if I want to go out with my friends.

Exercise 5 – listening (see page 17 and transcript 4)

A 1. disputes 2. exemple 3. ménagers 4. vaisselle 5. chambre 6. gronde 7. émissions 8. regardent

B 1. entends 2. sont 3. amis 4. critiquent 5. boîte 6. dix-sept 7. enfant 8. privée

C 1. dispute 2. éducation 3. week-ends 4. magasin 5. argent 6. trouvent 7. étudier 8. dépensier

Exercise 6 (see page 18)

faire le ménage	mettre la table	passer l'aspirateur
faire le repassage	sortir la poubelle	faire son lit
faire le jardinage	faire la lessive	faire la cuisine

TOPIC 3 Ideal Parents – Les Parents Idéaux

Exercise 7a – listening (see page 20 and transcript 5)

Good parents

1 Ils s'occupent de leurs enfants.

2 Ils s'intéressent à l'éducation de leurs enfants.

3 Ils donnent de bons conseils à leurs enfants.

4 Ils traitent tous leurs enfants de la même façon.

5 Ils sont très compréhensifs et parlent de tout avec leurs enfants.

6 Ils font des excursions ensemble.

7 Ils apprennent les bonnes manières, la politesse et le respect des valeurs morales aux enfants.

Bad parents

1 Ils sont toujours en train de râler.

2 Ils partent souvent en vacances sans leurs enfants.

3 Ils sont très sévères.

4 Ils laissent leurs enfants tout faire.

5 Ils battent leurs enfants.

6 Ils gâtent leurs enfants.

Exercise 7b – translation (see page 20 and transcript 5)

Good parents

1 They take care of their children.

2 They are interested in their children's education.

3 They give good advice to their children.

4 They treat all their children in the same way.

5 They are understanding and speak about everything with their children.

6 They go on trips together.

7 They teach their children to have good manners, be polite and respect moral values.

Bad parents

1 They are always shouting.

2 They often go on holiday without their children.

3 They are very strict.

4 They let/allow their children to do anything.

5 They hit their children.

6 They spoil their children.

Exercise 8 – listening and translation (see page 20 and transcript 6)

Stéphanie

Her parents are the ideal parents because they are funny, nice and generous. They respect her private life and encourage her during difficult times.

Christophe

Parents should show proof of trust, patience and love. They should be fair and never nasty.

Thomas

Ideal parents should treat all their children the same. They should give them good advice and provide support and love which all children require/need.

TOPIC 4   Holidays with or without Parents? – Les Vacances avec ou sans Parents?

Exercise 9 translation (see page 22 and transcript 9)

Les avantages

They pay for everything we want.

You feel safer.

We can go on excursions together.

They take us to restaurants.

They look after us.

They carry the cases.

They take care of all the papers/documents.

Les inconvénients

They don't enjoy themselves in the same way.

They don't let us do anything on our own.

You've got to go with them all the time.

We don't like the same things.

You've always to ask permission if you want to go to a club.

We argue more often.

They can be embarrassing.

TOPIC 5   Ideal Holidays/Tourism – Les Vacances Idéales/Le Tourisme

Exercise 10 (see page 24)

Where would I spend my ideal holiday and why?

I would go to a hot country in winter to avoid/get away from the rain and cold in Glasgow.

I would like to go around the world to visit all the countries I am interested in.

My dream is to go to Japan to discover Japanese culture.

I would like to go a desert island to relax and take advantage of its peace and quiet/tranquillity.

I would really like to go to New York to visit all the monuments, walk in 'Central Park' and go shopping in all the luxurious shops/boutiques.

When?

Seasons – in winter, in summer, in autumn, in spring

Months – I would go in the month of January, February, etc.

Age – when I am older

With whom?

I would go with my best friend because we would have a great time together.

I think I would go with the family because I could take advantage of my parents' generosity and of course we'd have a very good holiday together.

I would go on holiday on my own because it's the best way to meet other people and do what you want.

Things you would do?

I would often go to restaurants to taste the specialities of the country.

I would visit a lot of famous monuments, art galleries, etc.

I would spend my days on the beach with a good book/novel.

I would do lots of sport like skiing, ice-skating and walking.

I would try to talk/speak with the locals/people from there to get to know their culture better and to improve my French, Spanish, German, etc.

Exercise 11 – listening (see page 24 and transcript 11)

	Name	Where?	Why?
1	Julien	Mexico	Windsurf and discover a country different from his own
2	Sylvie	Rome	Loves Italian culture and thinks Rome is one of the most beautiful cities
3	Farid	Ireland	Discover the beautiful countryside and traditions
4	Christine	Australia	Would love to spend Christmas and New Year on the beach (+ barbecue)

	When?	With whom?	What would they do?
1	doesn't say	his brother	2 weeks in the heart of Mexico 2 weeks on the beach
2	May – fewer tourists and it would be less hot	her family	See the Pope and go to mass. Visit the beautiful districts and eat in good restaurants
3	June – maybe less rain	alone	Bike rides – stopping in pubs and listening to traditional music whilst drinking Guinness
4	winter	her best friend	Visit the outback, coral reef, and watch handsome Australian men surfing. Buy presents in Sydney for her family and improve her English.

Test yourself (see page 25)

Exercise 12 – What do the following words mean?

- avoir de bon rapport avec quelqu'un   – *to have a good relationship with someone*
- bien s'entendre avec quelqu'un   – *to get on well with someone*
- méchant   – *nasty*
- avoir une sœur cadette   – *to have a younger sister*

- donner de bons conseils   –   *to give good advice*

- découvrir   –   *to discover*

- faire le repassage   –   *to do the ironing*

- tandis que   –   *at the same time, meanwhile*

- afin de   –   *in order to*

Exercise 13 – Complete the sentences using the correct form of the adjectives given:

Mes parents sont très disponibles.

Ma sœur est toujours très énervante.

Mes frères sont fainéants.

Ma grand-mère est vieille mais vive.

Mon père est marrant/drôle.

Mon frère est quelquefois agressif.

Ma mère est tolérante.

Mes sœurs sont compréhensives.

Exercise 14 – Translate the following sentences:

I often argue/have arguments with my younger sister.

Parents should not spoil their children.

Having had breakfast, I brushed my teeth.

I would go on holiday with my parents because we get on well together.

I would like to go to a hot country in the winter so as to avoid the cold and rain in Scotland.

TOPIC 6   Home Area – Chez Soi

Exercise 15 – listening and translation (see pages 27 and 28)

Living in town – positive aspects (see transcript 12)

Il y a beaucoup de choses à faire et à voir.

– *There are a lot of things to do and see.*

Il y a énormément de divertissements à proximité.

– *There are lots of forms of entertainment nearby/close at hand.*

On n'est pas obligé d'avoir une voiture car il y a de bons transports en commun.

– *You don't need a car because public transport is good.*

Living in town – negative aspects (see transcript 12)

Il y a beaucoup de voitures et par conséquent trop de pollution.

- *There are lots of cars and therefore too much pollution.*

La vie en ville peut être stressante à cause du bruit et de la circulation.

- Town life can be stressful because of the noise and traffic.

Il n'y a pas assez d'espaces verts.

- There are not enough green areas.

Il y a trop de monde en ville et par conséquent on est toujours stressé.

- There are too many people in town and therefore you are always stressed.

Les loyers en ville sont très élevés et c'est donc très difficile de trouver un appartement convenable.

- The price of renting is very high in town and it is therefore very difficult to find a suitable flat.

On peut se sentir seul car il y a un fort anonymat en ville.

- You can feel alone because there is a strong feeling of anonymity/being anonymous in the town.

Il y a beaucoup de crime en ville et donc on ne se sent pas toujours en sécurité.

- There is a lot of crime in town and therefore you don't always feel safe.

Living in the country – positive aspects (see transcript 13)

Tout le monde connaît ses voisins alors on ne se sent jamais seul.

- Everyone knows their neighbours so you never feel alone.

C'est très agréable pour les enfants parce que les parents peuvent les laisser jouer dehors sans s'inquiéter.

- It is very pleasant for children because their parents can leave them to play outside without worrying/any worries.

On peut profiter de la nature et de la tranquillité.

- You can make the most of nature and the tranquillity/peace and quiet.

Les gens sont moins stressés à la campagne et on arrive à mieux se détendre.

- People are less stressed in the country and it is easier to relax.

Il n'y a pas beaucoup de circulation et par conséquent peu de bruit et de pollution.

- There is not a lot of traffic and therefore little noise and pollution.

L'air est pur et on peut se promener tranquillement dans les champs sans se sentir étouffé par le bruit et la saleté en ville.

- The air is pure and you can walk peacefully in the fields without feeling suffocated by the noise and dirt of town.

Living in the country – negative aspects (see transcript 13)

Il y a peu de possibilités de travail, alors beaucoup de jeunes quittent la campagne pour aller chercher du travail en ville.

- There are few employment possibilities so many young people leave the country to look for work in town.

Il n'y a rien aux alentours et on s'ennuie facilement.

- There is nothing in the area and you get bored easily.

Tout le monde est toujours au courant de tout ce qu'on fait ce qui peut parfois être gênant.

- Everyone always knows everything about what you are doing and that can be annoying sometimes.

La campagne n'est pas bien desservie par les transports en commun et il faut donc souvent avoir une voiture pour se déplacer.

- The country is not very well served by public transport/the country does not have good public transport links and therefore you often need a car to get around.

Living by the sea – positive aspects (see transcript 14)

On se sent toujours en vacances parce que la plage est à proximité.

- You always feel like you're on holiday because the beach is nearby.

Lorsqu'il fait beau on peut passer ses journées à la plage sans dépenser d'argent.

- When it is a nice day you can spend your day at the beach without spending any money.

Il y a toujours beaucoup de travail en été pour les étudiants.

- There is always a lot of work for students in the summer.

Le paysage est vraiment beau malgré le temps.

- The scenery is really beautiful in spite of the weather.

On peut faire beaucoup de sports aquatiques ce qui est vraiment super.

- You can do a lot of water sports which is really great.

Le bruit de la mer est très paisible et aide à se détendre.

- The sound of the sea is very peaceful and helps you relax.

Living by the sea – negative aspects (see transcript 14)

Les voitures sont vite rouillées à cause de l'air marin.

- Cars become rusty quickly because of the sea air.

Les odeurs de poisson et de la mer peuvent parfois être désagréables.

- The smell of fish and the sea can be unpleasant sometimes.

Il y a souvent du brouillard ce qui peut être très dangereux pour conduire.

- There is often fog which can be dangerous for driving/can make driving dangerous.

En hiver la mer est souvent très agitée et ça peut être très dangereux.

- In the winter the sea is often very rough and that can be very dangerous.

En été il y a beaucoup de touristes et les résidents de la ville se plaignent des encombrements qu'ils provoquent.

- In the summer there are a lot of tourists and the town residents complain about the traffic jams they create.

Test yourself (see page 30)

Exercise 16 – What do the following words mean?

- les divertissements — *entertainment*
- s'inquiéter — *to worry*
- s'ennuyer — *to get bored*
- les transports en commun — *public transport*

- les loyers   – *the rent*

- aux alentours   – *around/about/in the vicinity*

- gênant   – *disturbing/embarrassing*

- se détendre   – *to relax*

- la rouille   – *rust*

Exercise 17 – Translate the following sentences into English:

1 I like living in town because it is livelier/busier than the country.

2 Life in the country is quiet and relaxing.

3 There is too much pollution in town because of all the vehicles.

4 I would not like to live in the country because it is too isolated.

5 I would not like to live by the sea because I am frightened of water.

6 Life in the country is too boring.

7 There is a lot of crime in town and therefore it is dangerous.

Exercise 18 – Correct the word(s) underlined (see page 30)

Il y a beaucoup <u>de la</u> circulation en ville.
(de – after 'beaucoup' always 'de')

Il n'y a pas assez <u>des</u> divertissements à la campagne.
(de – after 'assez')

Il y a un grand nombre <u>des</u> restaurants en ville.
(de – after 'un grand nombre')

Il y a peu <u>des</u> choses <u>intéressant</u> à faire à la campagne.
(de – after 'peu' and 'intéressantes' as 'choses' is feminine and plural)

La vie est <u>cherer</u> en ville qu'à la campagne.
(plus chère – in French we use 'plus' + adjective for comparisons)

TOPIC 7 **Leisure and Healthy Living – Les Loisirs et La Santé**

Exercise 19a – listening (see page 32 and transcript 18)

1 Pour être en bonne santé, il faut manger beaucoup de fruits et de légumes et faire un peu de sport.

2 Pour se maintenir en forme, on doit manger équilibré et faire du sport, comme jouer au foot ou faire de la natation.

3 Pour garder la ligne, il faut surtout boire beaucoup d'eau, manger sainement et faire de l'exercice.

4 Ce qui est bon pour la santé, c'est de manger à des heures régulières et d'avoir une alimentation riche en vitamine.

5 A mon avis le secret d'une bonne santé, c'est de faire du sport tous les jours et de manger ce dont on a envie.

Exercise 19b – translation (see page 32 and transcript 18)

1 To be in good health, you need to eat a lot of fruit and vegetables and do a little sport.

2 To stay in good shape you have to eat a balanced diet and do some sport like playing football or going swimming.

3 To keep your figure, you have above all to drink a lot of water, eat healthily and do exercise.

4 What is good for your health is to eat at regular times and have a diet rich in vitamins.

5 In my opinion the secret of good health is to do some sport every day and eat what you want.

Exercise 20a (see page 32)

Il ne faut pas grignoter entre les repas parce que ça fait grossir.

On ne devrait pas boire trop de boissons sucrées car le sucre est très mauvais pour les dents et peut créer des caries.

Il ne faut pas trop manger le soir parce que ça nous empêche de bien dormir.

Une nourriture trop grasse est nuisible à la santé et peut provoquer les problèmes de cholestérol.

Il ne faut pas sauter les repas car on a besoin de la nourriture pour apporter de l'énergie à notre corps.

Il ne faut pas beaucoup manger avant de faire du sport car la nourriture a besoin d'être bien digérée pour éviter les crampes.

Si on ne fait pas de sport on devient fainéant et le corps se rouille.

Il faut toujours s'échauffer avant de faire du sport pour ne pas se déchirer les muscles et pour éviter les courbatures.

Exercise 20b – translation (see page 32)

You shouldn't snack between meals because that makes you put on weight/become fat.

You shouldn't drink too many sweet drinks because sugar is very bad for your teeth and can cause tooth decay.

You shouldn't eat too much in the evening because it will prevent you from sleeping well/getting a good night's sleep.

Foods which are too fatty harm your health and can create/cause cholesterol problems.

You shouldn't skip meals because your body needs food for energy.

You shouldn't eat a lot before doing sport because food needs to be well digested to avoid you getting cramp.

If you don't do sport you become lazy and the body becomes rusty.

You should always warm up before doing sport so as to avoid pulling a muscle and being sore/stiff.

Exercise 21a – listening (see page 33 and transcript 19)

Les gens fument/boivent trop d'alcool/prennent de la drogue ...
... pour échapper à la réalité
... pour avoir l'air cool
... pour oublier les problèmes familiaux
... par souci d'appartenance à un groupe social
... parce qu'ils sont influencés par les amis
... à cause du stress de la société
... pour perdre du poids
... pour faire comme les autres/les amis/les parents
... pour le plaisir.

Exercise 21b – translation (see page 33 and transcript 19)

People smoke/drink too much alcohol/take drugs ...
... to escape reality
... to look cool
... to forget family problems
... through wanting to belong to a social group
... because they are influenced by their friends
... because of stress in society
... to lose weight
... to be like everyone else/friends/parents
... for enjoyment.

Exercise 22 – translation (see page 34 and transcript 20)

The Effects of Smoking

Nicotine is very harmful for your blood circulation.
It harms the body and health.

Smoking is harmful for smokers as well as non-smokers.
Smoke stings the eyes and pollutes the air.

Cigarettes are responsible for serious illnesses such as asthma/heart problems/cancer.
Cigarettes make the skin look grey and cause premature ageing.

Cigarettes give you bad breath and make your teeth yellow.
Smokers often have yellow fingers.

Exercise 23 – translation (see page 35 and transcript 21)

The Effects of Alcohol

Alcohol doesn't have any particular nutritional value and can make you put on weight.
Alcohol gives you bad breath.
Drinking alcohol in an irresponsible way can be dangerous for you as well as your loved ones.

Alcohol affects the brain and weakens our physical and mental faculties.
You no longer know what you are doing when you drink too much alcohol.
Too much alcohol often makes people violent.

Too much alcohol causes serious illness such as heart diseases/cancer of the liver.

Exercise 24 – translation (see page 36 and transcript 22)

The Effects of Drug Use

Drugs affect our reflexes.
Drugs are very dangerous for the brain and blood circulation.
Taking drugs can lead to serious illnesses.

Drugs can cost a lot.
Drugs and crime are often linked.

Certain drugs lead to addiction/dependency.
Drugs can turn a human being into a wreck.
There comes a time when it is difficult to do without them.

Drugs affect our social behaviour.
Normal life deteriorates.
It sometimes leads to a life of solitude.

Exercise 25 – translation (see page 37 and transcript 23)

We need to have more advertising campaigns exposing the dangers of drugs/smoking/alcohol.

Parents and schools need to be encouraged to talk to young people about the dangers as early as possible.

We need to speak more openly about them and stress the harmful affects of drugs/smoking/alcohol.

We should forbid/ban billboard advertising.

Exercise 26 – listening (see page 37 to 38 and transcript 24)

1 a healthy diet, some exercise/sport and avoiding drugs such as cigarettes and alcohol

2 false – he doesn't eat a lot of fatty food

3 sugary foods such as sweets and chocolate

4 false – he has to force himself to go to the swimming pool twice a week

5 He thinks that people do it to be part of a social group.

6 His grandfather smoked all his life and died of lung cancer last year at the age of 71.

7 school, youth clubs and TV

8 We would have a better quality of life, be happier and live longer.

Test yourself (see page 39)

Exercise 27 – What do the following words mean?

- une alimentation variée   – *a varied diet*
- une nourriture saine   – *healthy food*
- être en bonne santé   – *to be in good health*
- une vie saine   – *a healthy life*
- faire un régime   – *to go on a diet*
- prendre de la drogue   – *to take drugs*
- néfaste   – *harmful*
- les poumons   – *lungs*
- les substances nocives   – *harmful substances*

Exercise 28 – Translate the following sentences into English:

1 A balanced diet enables/allows us to stay in good health.

2 To keep in good form you need to have a healthy diet and do some sport.

3 You shouldn't skip meals if you don't want to lose you energy.

4 We can allow ourselves to eat rich food from time to time.

5 It is necessary to do some sport such as aerobics if you want to keep your figure.

6 Sport is a good way of relaxing and keeping fit/on form/in good health.

7 A lot of people start smoking to do as their friends are doing.

8 Some people smoke to fight against stress.

9 Smoking leads to/causes a lot of serious illnesses.

10 I would not like to feel dependent on a drug.

11 You should drink alcohol in moderation. If not it can be very dangerous.

12 Our society must do more to dissuade young people from taking drugs.

Exercise 29 – Correct the word(s) underlined:

Il faut manger <u>beacoup</u> de légumes et de fruits.
(beaucoup – watch the spelling of this word)

Une nourriture <u>sain</u> est indispensable pour rester en pleine forme.
(saine – nourriture is feminine)

Je <u>fait</u> beaucoup de sport pour me maintenir en forme.
(fais – is the 'je' form)

Il y a un grand nombre <u>des</u> personnes qui <u>fume</u> de plus en plus jeune.
(de – after un grand nombre, fument – the plural third person)

TOPIC 8 Television and Films – La Télévision et Les Films

Exercise 30 – translation (see page 41)

every day
at the weekends
never
when it is raining

Exercise 31 – listening (see page 41 and transcript 27)

1 rarement
2 assez souvent
3 de temps en temps quand il y a quelque chose d'intéressant
4 en général – pendant les vacances – pendant des heures
5 quand je m'ennuie

Exercise 32 – translation (see page 41)

I prefer watching nature programmes because I find them interesting and you can learn a lot from them.

I love soaps and could never miss them. You always want to know what will happen next.

What I like watching on TV are films, in particular foreign films which are subtitled. They allow me to listen to another language and see other actors who are not known in the UK.

Exercise 33a – listening (see page 41 and transcript 28)

1 regarder – informations – permet – mondiaux
2 dessins animés – marrants – routine
3 émissions de sport – beaucoup de sport – motive

Exercise 33b – translation (see page 41 and transcript 28)

1 I only like watching the news on TV because it allows me to be informed about world events.

2 I love cartoons because they are very funny and help us to escape from our everyday routine.

3 I like watching sports programmes a lot, especially athletics. I do a lot of sport and seeing the professionalism of these people motivates me more.

Exercise 34 – translation (see page 41)

What I can't stand watching on TV are the cartoons, I find them ridiculous and they teach us nothing of any importance.

I hate game shows on TV; there are far too many and I think the money won by the contestants could help others who need it more.

I never watch films on TV because I prefer to see them in the cinema on a big screen. It makes the film more captivating and creates a more realistic atmosphere.

Exercise 35a – listening (see pages 41 to 42 and transcript 29)

1 feuilletons – jamais – s'arrêter – drogue
2 documentaires – intéressants – embarrassants
3 émissions comiques – drôles – faux rires – présente – beaucoup

Exercise 35b – translation (see pages 41 to 42 and transcript 29)

1 I hate soap operas on TV and I never watch them. As soon as you start watching them you can no longer stop. It is really like a drug

2 I find it really hard to watch biographical documentaries. I find them uninteresting and sometimes a little embarrassing.

3 I hate comedy programmes because I don't find them at all funny. Moreover/in addition you have to listen to the forced laughter of an audience which is not even present and to be quite honest, it really gets on my nerves.

Exercise 36 – translation (see page 42 and transcript 30)

Positive Aspects

TV is a good way of ...
... discovering new horizons
... discovering other cultures
... relaxing (after school).

There are programmes for all tastes such as ...
... cartoons
... soaps
... sports programmes

... game shows
... music programmes.

TV teaches us things about ...
... other countries
... science
... nature.

It is a good form of communication.
It is an extraordinary means of communication.

It is educational ...
... TV informs us.
... TV entertains us.
... TV teaches us.
... TV educates us.

TV plays a cultural role. It gives us access to ...
... music
... culture
... history.

Exercise 37 – translation (see page 43 and transcript 31)

Negative aspects

We risk becoming lethargic/sluggish.
We risk becoming couch potatoes.

Certain people cannot live without television.
There are too many people who spend their life in front of 'the small screen'.

TV makes us stupid.
TV makes us soft.
TV makes us lazy.
TV can prevent people from doing other more interesting things.

TV has a tendency to put a stop to communication.
People no longer talk to one another.

There are too many ...
... stupid programmes
... game shows
... silly programmes
... programmes of mediocre quality
... cartoons.
TV is full of stupid and useless adverts.

Certain programmes are stupid.
There are too many soaps and each one is more stupid than the other.
Certain series never end.

Test yourself (see page 43)

Exercise 38 – What do the following words mean?

- les dessins animés — *cartoons*
- les feuilletons — *soap operas*
- de temps en temps — *sometimes/from time to time*
- les jeux — *game shows*
- les informations — *the news*
- jardiner — *to do the gardening*
- le grand écran — *the big screen*
- éducatif — *educational*
- briser la communication — to *break/to stop communication*
- se passionner pour — *to have a passion for/to be fascinated by*

Exercise 39 – Translate the following sentences into English:

In my opinion television is an extraordinary means of communication.

Television teaches us a lot about other countries and cultures.

Television helps me to relax after a long day at school.

In my opinion, television always shows the same type of programmes.

A lot of people watch too much TV and cannot do without it.

In my opinion there are too many useless and stupid programmes on television.

Exercise 40 – Put the following sentences into a negative form:

Je regarde la télé quand il fait beau. (never)

Je ne regarde jamais la télé quand il fait beau.

J'aime regarder les émissions de sports. (only)

Je n'aime regarder que les émissions de sports.

Je regarde les feuilletons tous les jours. (no longer)

Je ne regarde plus les feuilletons tous les jours.

Il y a beaucoup d'émissions intéressantes à la télé. (not)

Il n'y a pas beaucoup d'émissions intéressantes à la télé.

J'aime les feuilletons et les films. (neither nor)

Je n'aime ni les feuilletons ni les films.

TOPIC 1 School and Teachers – Le Lycée et Les Professeurs

Exercise 41 – Qualities of teachers (see page 45 and transcript 32)

A good teacher is one who is ...
... serious
... patient
... ready to help/helpful
... conscientious
... warm
... fair.

A good teacher is one who ...
... explains everything clearly
... gives the necessary help
... prepares his/her lessons well

A good teacher has ...
... a good sense of humour.

A bad teacher is one who ...
... is not patient
... doesn't explain anything
... has no sense of humour.

A good school is one which has ...
... a nice atmosphere
... a good success rate in exams
... discipline
... good relations between the pupils and teachers.

A good school is one where ...
... the pupils want to succeed
... the teachers are always available
... there is no violence.

A good school is one which ...
... signals any absences
... protects its pupils
... is well equipped.

Exercise 42 – listening (see page 46 and transcript 33)

Qu'est-ce qu'un bon prof?

Un bon enseignant ...
... est juste et équitable avec tout le monde
... a un très bon sens de l'humour
... apporte une aide nécessaire lorsque quelqu'un en a besoin
... explique sa matière de façon claire et précise en donnant des exemples.

Qu'est-ce qu'un mauvais prof?

Un mauvais prof ...
... a un chouchou dans chaque classe
... donne seulement des exercices sans les expliquer.

Qu'est-ce qu'une bonne école?

Une bonne école ...
   ... a un personnel compétent qui est toujours prêt à aider
   ... implique les élèves dans la vie scolaire
   ... est un endroit sûr où l'on peut se promener sans danger
   ... propose des activités parascolaires intéressantes pour les élèves.

TOPIC 2   School Uniform – L'Uniforme

Exercise 43 – translation

Advantages (see page 47 and transcript 34)

It allows us to distinguish those people not belonging to the school.

Uniform reduces the differences between pupils.
You don't waste time looking for what you are going to wear for the day.

You can take a certain pride in wearing uniform.

It is smart and can cost less than designer clothes.

It distinguishes us from other schools.
You feel part of a social group.

Wearing uniform allows us to be better equipped for the world of work.

Disadvantages (see page 48 and transcript 35)

It is not comfortable for working.
In summer you are too hot and in winter you are too cold.

You lose your individuality.
Everyone is dressed the same.

It is not practical for playing.

It can create arguments/conflicts between schools.

You are obliged to buy clothes that you don't necessarily like.

TOPIC 3   Subject Choice – Le Choix des Matières

Exercise 44 – translation (see page 49 and transcript 36)

I am really interested in music and therefore have decided to study it this year.

I have decided to study sport this year because I am very sporty and I would like to be a PE teacher one day.

I have chosen IT because I think that nowadays it is very important to know how to master technology.

I love reading and poetry therefore I have chosen English to develop my knowledge further.

I have chosen maths this year because I think that it is indispensable for everyday life.

I have chosen maths and physics because I think that they are two fundamental subjects to better explain the world around us.

Exercise 45a – listening (see page 49 and transcript 37)

Je trouve que c'est très important d'étudier une langue étrangère car on devient plus tolérant envers d'autres cultures.

Le fait d'étudier une langue étrangère nous aide à mieux comprendre notre propre langue.

Une langue étrangère nous permet de communiquer avec les gens de différents pays.

J'ai choisi le français car je veux étudier les langues à la faculté.

A mon avis, les langues étrangères sont indispensables pour l'Union Européenne.

Exercise 45b – translation (see page 49 and transcript 37)

I think that it is important to study a foreign language because you become more tolerant towards other cultures.

Studying a foreign language helps us to understand our own language better.

A foreign language allows us/enables us to communicate with people from different countries.

I have chosen French because I want to study languages at university.

In my opinion foreign languages are indispensable for the EU.

TOPIC 4 Future Aspirations – Aspirations Futures

Exercise 46 – grammar (see page 51)

Infinitive	Future	Conditional
pouvoir	il pourra	il pourrait
vouloir	il voudra	il voudrait
voir	il verra	il verrait
venir	il viendra	il viendrait

Exercise 47 – Test yourself (see pages 52 to 53)

1 c

2 c

3 a

4 c – it should be 'ils aimeraient'

5 d – with 'quand' the first clause needs to be in future

6 b

7 b – (remember 'à l'étranger' means 'abroad' not 'stranger')

8 b – (remember 'réussir à un examen' means 'to pass an exam', 'passer un examen' means 'to sit an exam')

Exercise 48 – translation (see pages 53 to 54 and transcript 38)

Go to University

When I leave school I would like to go to university to study ... because I want to be ...

If I pass my exams, I will go to Glasgow University to study law.

Go abroad

One day I would like to live abroad because I am really interested in other cultures.

When I leave school, I would like to go to France to get to know the traditions and country better and to improve my French.

A gap year

When I leave school, I would like to take a gap year to rest.

Next year when I leave school, I would like to take a gap year and do some voluntary work.

Look for a job

After my Highers, I would like to start working immediately to earn some money.

When I leave school, I would like to find a job because I want to have my own flat and independence.

Stay at home or leave

I would prefer to stay at home during my studies because all the comforts for studying are here and that would allow me to spend less money.

I would like to go to university in another town because I want to take advantage of student life.

As soon as I find work I will move out because I don't get on very well with my parents.

I will stay at home for as long as possible because I am close to my family and I am a little frightened/scared of living far from them.

Don't know

I don't know what I want to do when I leave school. In fact it scares me a little.

At the moment I don't know what I will do when I leave school but I am not too worried about it.

Exercise 49 – reading/translation (see pages 54 to 56)

1 Christophe

2 Christine

3 Thomas

4 Sylvie

5 Julien

6 Christine

7 Julien

8 Christophe

Exercise 50 – translation (see page 56)

At present/at the moment I am preparing for my exams which I will take/sit in two months. I love history because it teaches us a lot about our ancestors and our present life/our life as it is today.

At the moment, I do not really know what I want to do next year but I am going to have to decide soon/I will need to decide soon as it is beginning to cause tension within the family.

Test yourself (see page 57)

Exercise 51 – What do the following words mean?

- enseigner   – *to teach*

- un lycée   – *a secondary school*

- apprendre   – *to learn/to teach*

- un pion   – *a person who looks after the pupils*

- échouer à un examen   – *to fail an exam*

- passer un examen   – *to sit/to take an exam*

- les matières   – *subjects*

- les langues étrangères   – *foreign languages*

Exercise 52 – Translate the following sentences into English:

A good teacher is someone who listens to the pupils.

A good teacher is always fair and available/there for you.

A good school rarely has discipline problems/problems with discipline.

A good school has a warm/welcoming atmosphere.

I am really interested in foreign languages.

I really love/I have a passion for music.

I am studying French this year because I think that foreign languages are important for my career.

Exercise 53 – Look at the following sentences and correct the underlined words:

Quand je <u>quitterais</u> l'école j'aimerais être avocat.

(quitterais – quitterai, as this is a future idea)

Un bon prof est celui qui <u>expliquet</u> tous clairement.

(expliquet – explique as this is the correct form of 'expliquer' in third person singular)

Un mauvais prof est celui qui est trop <u>sévères</u> et <u>stricts</u>.

(sévères – sévère and stricts – strict – the noun is singular therefore no 's' is required)

Je ne <u>sait</u> pas si je <u>veut</u> aller à la fac.

(sait – sais, veut – veux, sais and veux are the correct forms in the first person singular)

Une <u>bon</u> école est <u>une</u> endroit <u>ou</u> on se sent en sécurité.

(bon – bonne, as school is feminine, une – un as 'endroit' is masculine, ou – où as ou means 'or' not 'where')

Exercise 54 – The Grammar Quiz (see pages 60 to 61)

1 c   – it should read 'pendant les grandes vacances nous sommes allés en France'

2 false   – reflexive verbs and most verbs of movement take être

3 d   – 'elles' is feminine and plural so it needs an extra 'e' and 's' with the verb être

4 false

5 d   – a should read – 'l'hôtel se trouvait en face d'une grande place'

           – b should read 'nous nous promenions tous les jours'

           – c should read 'la chambre donnait sur un lac'

6 a   – the past participle of 'boire' is 'bu'

Exercise 55 – listening and translation (see page 63 and transcript 39)

1 Last year I went to Paris with a group of twenty people.

2 During the Christmas holidays I went to France with my best friend.

3 Last summer I spent two weeks in Brittany with school.

4 During the Easter holidays, our school took part in a school exchange in France.

5 Last year I worked for a month in a hotel in Toulouse in the south-west of France.

6 During the summer holidays I was lucky to spend a month in Lyon in France at my pen friend's house.

Exercise 56a – listening (see page 66 and transcript 40)

1   long, ennuyeux, vraiment, affreux, vieille, jolie, génial, amusé

2   super, amusant, cher, sale, propre, moderne, pratique, super, grande, équipée

3   vraiment, magnifique, ennuyeux, long, très sympa, super, très joli, spacieuse, moderne

4   long, très confortable, pratique, vieille, sale, petites, peu confortables, content

Exercise 56b – translation (see page 66 and transcript 40)

1   Last summer I went to Brittany in the north of France with the school. We went by coach to Dover and then got the ferry to Calais. After that the coach took us to our destination in Brittany. The trip/journey was long and boring and I was ill on the ferry. It was really awful/terrible. Once we arrived, we went to the youth hostel which was situated in a small village. It was old but really pretty. In addition/moreover/furthermore I had to share the room with my best friend. It was great and we really enjoyed ourselves.

2   During the Easter holidays, I was lucky to find a job in a hotel in Paris in France. I took the plane from Glasgow airport on Saturday morning and arrived in Paris at lunchtime. The journey/trip was great and really funny because it was the first time that I had taken the plane. Once I had arrived in Paris, I took the métro to the sixteenth district where my hotel was. The métro wasn't expensive but it was really dirty. I was a little frightened/scared. The hotel, however, was very clean and modern. It was really practical because it was five minutes away from the Eiffel tower. It was great. I had my own room which was really big and very well equipped. I felt at ease immediately.

3   A year ago, during the Christmas holidays, I took part in a school exchange. We went to Grenoble in the Alps for a week and it was really amazing/magnificent. We left Glasgow by train on Sunday morning and arrived in Grenoble on Monday at lunchtime. The trip/journey was boring because it was very long and it was cold in the carriages. At Grenoble train station, the host families were waiting for us to take us back to their house. It was really nice of them. My host family's house was great. It was like a Swiss chalet and had a beautiful view of the Alps. It was really pretty. The house was spacious and modern and I even had my own room.

4   During the summer holidays, I went to Provence in France with the school. There were/we were twenty pupils and three teachers. We left Glasgow on the coach at one o'clock in the morning and then we took the Eurostar to arrive in France at two o'clock the next afternoon. We then continued our journey by coach to our destination of Provence. The journey/trip didn't seem very long because the coach was comfortable and we were able to sleep. The Eurostar was very practical as well. We stayed in a youth hostel in Provence which was in the heart of the countryside. The youth hostel was very old and quite dirty. Moreover/in addition/furthermore the bedrooms were very small and uncomfortable. We were not very happy with our accommodation.

Exercise 57 – reading (see pages 68 to 69)

Stéphanie	Christophe	Thomas
F, F, T, F	F, F, T, F	T, F, T, F

Exercise 58 – translation (see page 69)

Stéphanie

Last year I worked as a waitress in a hotel in Grenoble. I was responsible for taking customers' orders and for lunch service. I got on really well with my colleagues. They were really nice/kind and helped me a lot with the work and the language and consequently I improved my French a lot. The town of Grenoble was very pretty with lots of cafés where we had a drink after work.

Christophe

Last summer I went to France where I spent two weeks at my pen friend's house. His house was not very big therefore I didn't have my own room. His family were very welcoming and we did a lot together. As the town was neither very pretty nor very big, we went on a lot of excursions in the area and one time we went to Paris.

Thomas

Last May, I took part in an exchange with my school. We went to France for two weeks. The school in France was not as big as my school in Scotland and it was also very old. The host family were great and really kind/nice and I really felt at home. The only disadvantage was that there wasn't a lot to do in the town but we enjoyed ourselves nevertheless.

Exercise 59a – listening (see page 73 and transcript 41)

1 free time activities

sunny days

spent time on the beach playing volley-ball

swimming

met good-looking French boys

went on some excursions

in the evening ate in restaurants

food

really good

specialities: fish and seafood

was able to eat them everyday

2 free time activities

went on nice walks in the old town

took lovely photos

in the evening went to night-clubs

in the evening had a drink in a café

food

not good

ate the same thing everyday

too fatty or too cold

3 free time activities

Saturday:

went skiing

went snowboarding

Sunday:

stayed in hotel

ate in hotel

in the afternoon went to the small town

bought some presents for friends in Scotland

food

ate a raclette, a speciality of the region

delicious

Exercise 59b – translation (see page 73 and transcript 41)

Last summer I went to Brittany in France with the school. We were there for a week and stayed in a youth hostel which was 200 metres from the beach. It was great. On sunny days we spent a lot of time on the beach playing volleyball and swimming. We even met some good-looking French boys. They were really nice. We also went on some excursions to visit the region. In the evening we ate in restaurants. The food was really good. The specialities of Brittany are fish and seafood and I was able to eat some everyday.

Last year, during the Easter holidays I went to Lyon in the east of France. I worked there as a waiter in a big hotel for a month and I had my own bedroom in the hotel. When I wasn't working, I went on lovely walks through the old town. The architecture in Lyon is really beautiful and I was able to take lots of lovely photos. In the evening I went either to a nightclub with my colleagues or we went out for a drink in a café. As I wasn't earning a lot of money, I had to eat in the staff canteen in the hotel. The food in the hotel was really not good. We ate the same thing everyday and it was too fatty or too cold.

Four weeks ago, I went to the Alps for a weekend with my parents. We hired a chalet with two bedrooms and a view over the ski slopes. It was beautiful/magnificent. On Saturday we went skiing and snowboarding. On Sunday morning we stayed in the hotel because it was snowing really hard and therefore we couldn't go out. At lunchtime we ate a 'raclette' which is one of the specialities of the region. It was really delicious. On Sunday afternoon we were able to go out and we went to the small town to buy some presents for our friends in Scotland. I spent/had an unforgettable weekend but it was a little short.

Lifestyles and the Wider World (see pages 90 to 92)

Family – La Famille

Je vais vous parler de mes opinions/avis sur mes relations familiales/rapports familiaux.

Je m'entends bien avec ma famille.

Je dois partager ma chambre avec ma sœur et je n'aime pas ça/ça ne me plaît pas.

Bien sûr/naturellement il y a souvent de petites disputes chez moi à propos de …

Nous nous disputons/on se dispute souvent à propos des tâches ménagères/du ménage, de mes devoirs, etc.

Je déteste ranger ma chambre. Elle est toujours en désordre et mes parents me grondent souvent (à ce propos).

J'aime vivre à la maison/chez moi.

J'ai été très bien élevé(e) et j'ai un bon rapport avec mes parents/je m'entends très bien avec mes parents.

Je me sens chez moi.

J'élèverais mes enfants de la même façon.

C'est très important d'être indépendant/d'avoir son indépendance.

J'aimerais avoir mon propre appartement pour pouvoir faire/afin de faire ce dont j'ai envie/ce que je veux.

J'aimerais quitter la maison/déménager car je m'entends mieux avec ma famille quand je suis loin d'elle.

Je n'aimerais pas quitter la maison/déménager car j'aurais tout le ménage à faire tout(e) seul(e)/je serais obligé(e) de faire le ménage moi-même.

Ma famille et mes amis me manqueraient si je déménageais.

Les parents idéaux sont – compréhensifs, aimables, strictes mais justes, marrants, serviables et bienveillants.

Friendship – L'Amitié

A mon avis, l'amitié est très importante.

Je fais confiance à mes amis et à ma famille.

Un bon ami/une bonne amie est quelqu'un sur qui on peut compter/à qui on peut faire confiance, et qui est marrant(e) et aimable.

Mes meilleurs amis/meilleures amies s'appellent …

Nous avons les mêmes goûts et intérêts.

J'aurais du mal à vivre/je ne pourrais pas me debrouiller sans mes amis.

Un bon ami est toujours là pour toi.

Ce que je ne supporte pas chez un ami c'est la jalousie.

Holidays with or without Parents? – Les Vacances avec ou sans Parents?

Je préfère aller en vacances avec mes parents car ils payent tout.

Je préfère aller en vacances avec mes amis au lieu de ma famille.

Il y a bien sûr des avantages et des inconvénients à aller en vacances avec ses parents/ses amis.

Chaque année, depuis mon enfance, je passe mes vacances avec mes parents.

J'adore aller en vacances/passer les vacances avec mes parents car ils sont jeunes d'esprit/ils ont une mentalité jeune.

Ils me donnent de l'argent lorsque/quand j'en ai besoin.

Je préférerais aller en vacances avec mes amis. On peut faire ce qu'on veut, quand on veut.

Je préférerais aller en vacances/passer les vacances avec mes amis mais mes parents pensent que je suis trop jeune pour me débrouiller seul(e).

Ideal Holidays/Tourism – Les Vacances Idéales/Le Tourisme

Mes vacances idéales seraient sur une île au soleil car j'adore la mer et la chaleur.

Mes vacances idéales seraient en Islande car c'est très intéressant et il y aurait beaucoup à voir et à faire.

L'Ecosse est un très beau pays, plein de traditions.

Il pleut beaucoup en Ecosse mais le paysage est vraiment beau/magnifique.

Le tourisme est très important en Ecosse.

Home Area – Chez Soi

J'adore vivre en ville car il y a beaucoup à y faire.

Tout est à proximité/est à portée de main.

La ville est toujours très animée car la vie nocturne est géniale.

Il y a beaucoup d'avantages et d'inconvénients à vivre en ville/à la campagne/au bord de la mer.

Il y a beaucoup de gens et de voitures en ville et par conséquent/donc beaucoup de pollution.

Il y a aussi beaucoup de bruit en ville/la ville est très bruyante.

La ville est polluée par les gaz d'échappements des voitures/les gaz d'échappements des voitures polluent la ville.

Je n'aimerais pas/je détesterais vivre en ville/à la campagne/au bord de la mer.

Si je vivais à la campagne, je m'ennuierais à mourir.

Je préférerais vivre en ville/au bord de la mer/à la campagne car ...

L'air est pur et propre à la campagne.

Si on vit/habite à la campagne, on peut faire beaucoup de (belles) promenades.

J'aimerais vivre à l'étranger pour apprendre (des choses sur) d'autres cultures/découvrir (des choses sur) différentes cultures.

Leisure and Healthy Living – Les Loisirs et La Santé

Avoir une vie saine est très important pour moi.

J'ai un régime équilibré/je mange équilibré/je mange sainement et je fais beaucoup de sport pour rester en forme.

Afin de rester en bonne santé/pour rester en bonne santé on devrait avoir un régime équilibré et faire du sport.

On ne devrait pas fumer car ça peut provoquer des cancers et d'autres maladies graves.

Fumer rend aussi la peau grise.

On ne devrait boire de l'alcool qu'avec modération.

Il faut boire beaucoup d'eau.

Malheureusement beaucoup de jeunes gens mangent, fument et boivent trop.

Beaucoup de jeunes prennent aussi le volant en ayant bu ce qui est très dangereux.

Television and Films – La Télévision et Les Films

J'adore regarder la télévision et aller au cinéma.

Mes émissions préférées/favorites sont les feuilletons et les documentaires.

La télévision peut être une bonne chose car on peut apprendre beaucoup sur différents pays.

A mon avis, la télévision peut être dangereuse car il y a trop d'émissions violentes et trop de publicité (à la télévision).

Je préfère aller au cinéma car j'aime regarder les films sur (un) grand écran.

Regarder des films français m'aide à améliorer mon français.

Education and Work (see page 92)

School and Teachers – Le Lycée et Les Professeurs

Un bon lycée/une bonne école doit/devrait avoir de bons profs.

Un bon lycée/une bonne école est celui/celle où les résultats sont bons, les élèves se sentent en sécurité et où il y a une bonne atmosphère.

Un bon prof est quelqu'un qui est – juste, compréhensif, patient, tolérant, marrant, serviable, qui a un bon sens de l'humour et qui ne donne pas trop de devoirs.

Par contre, un mauvais prof est quelqu'un qui est – toujours de mauvaise humeur, injuste et qui n'explique pas clairement.

Dans mon école on doit porter l'uniforme/il faut porter l'uniforme.

Ayant dit cela beaucoup d'élèves ne le portent pas.

A mon avis les élèves plus âgés ne devraient pas être obligés de porter l'uniforme.

Cette année à l'école, j'étudie cinq matières pour les Highers.

J'adore le sport et je suis membre de l'équipe de hockey à l'école.

Il y a de bons clubs dans notre école.

Future Aspirations – Aspirations Futures

L'année prochaine je vais rester à l'école/aller à la fac/aller à l'université/prendre une année sabbatique/trouver un emploi/trouver du travail.

Quand je quitterai l'école, j'aimerais aller à la fac/à l'université pour y étudier.

J'aimerais aussi aller en France pour améliorer/afin d'améliorer mon Français et apprendre plus sur les Français et leur culture.

J'aimerais vivre en France car j'ai entendu dire/il paraît/que les gens sont vraiment agréables et que la nourriture est délicieuse/bonne/excellente.

Career and Unemployment – Carrière et Chômage

J'aimerais être professeur car j'aime travailler avec les enfants.

Je veux/j'aimerais travailler en France car/parce que je veux découvrir une autre culture.

Je veux/J'aimerais pouvoir bien communiquer avec les Français.

Le chômage est un problème partout/global notamment à cause des nouvelles technologies et des ordinateurs qui ont remplacé l'homme.

L'ordinateur est une bonne chose car c'est rapide et cela réduit le taux de papier.

Listening Transcripts

Use this section along with the CD in order to:

- improve your listening comprehension

- improve your pronunciation

- select ideas and phrases for inclusion in your own speaking and writing.

Transcript 1 (see page 12)

Faire confiance à quelqu'un
exemple, Je fais confiance à ma sœur aînée.

Bien s'entendre avec quelqu'un
exemple, Je m'entends bien avec mes parents.

Se sentir proche de quelqu'un
exemple, Je me sens proche de mon frère cadet.

Se confier à quelqu'un
exemple, Je me confie toujours à ma meilleure amie.

Transcript 2 (see page 13)

J'ai une sœur et un frère mais je fais plus confiance à mon frère aîné car je sais qu'il peut garder un secret.

Je fais partie d'une famille nombreuse et je m'entends très bien avec tout le monde.

Je suis fille unique et donc je me sens très proche de mes parents.

Je me confie toujours à ma sœur jumelle car on est très proche l'un de l'autre.

TOPIC 2 Family Conflicts – Les Conflits Familiaux

Transcript 3 (see page 16)

avoir des disputes/des confrontations – *to have arguments*
  exemple, Il y a souvent des disputes à propos des travaux ménagers.
    Il y a souvent des confrontations à cause de l'argent.

se disputer – *to argue*
  exemple, Mes parents et moi nous disputons souvent à propos de mon petit ami/de ma petite amie.

se faire gronder par – *to be told off by*
  exemple, Je me fais toujours gronder par ma mère si je ne fais pas mes devoirs.

reprocher – *to criticise/to reproach*
  exemple, Mes parents me reprochent d'être trop effronté.

créer des tensions – *to create tensions*
  exemple, Il y a souvent des choses qui créent des tensions dans la famille.

ce qui m'énerve – *the thing that annoys me*
  exemple, Ce qui m'énerve chez mes parents c'est qu'il veulent tout savoir sur ma vie privée.

avoir besoin de demander la permission – *need to ask permission*
  exemple, J'ai toujours besoin de demander la permission si je veux sortir avec mes amis.

Transcript 4 (see page 17)

A De temps en temps il y a de petites disputes chez nous. Par exemple, moi, je n'aime pas faire les travaux ménagers comme faire la vaisselle ou passer l'aspirateur. Je ne range jamais ma chambre et par conséquent elle est toujours en désordre. Ma mère me gronde assez souvent à ce propos. En plus je n'aime ni les émissions de télévision que mes parents regardent ni la même nourriture et ceci peut créer énormément de tensions entre nous.

B Je ne m'entends pas toujours très bien avec mes parents car j'estime qu'ils sont trop sévères avec moi. On a souvent des confrontations à propos de mes sorties et de mes amis. Cependant, ce qui m'énerve le plus chez eux c'est qu'ils critiquent mes amis et m'empêchent souvent d'aller en boîte avec eux. J'ai dix-sept ans mais ils s'obstinent quand même à me traiter comme un enfant et s'occupent trop de ma vie privée, ce qui est trop injuste.

C En général je m'entends très bien avec mes parents mais parfois on se dispute à propos de mon éducation et de l'argent. Tous les week-ends je travaille dans un magasin de vêtements pour gagner un peu d'argent, mais mes parents trouvent que je devrais passer mes week-ends à étudier pour l'école. Je suis très dépensier (dépensière) aussi, ce qui les énerve d'autant plus.

TOPIC 3 Ideal Parents – Les Parents Idéaux

Transcript 5 (see page 20)

De bons parents:

Ils s'occupent de leurs enfants.

Ils s'intéressent à l'éducation de leurs enfants.

Ils donnent de bons conseils à leurs enfants.

Ils traitent tous leurs enfants de la même façon.

Ils sont très compréhensifs et parlent de tout avec leurs enfants.

Ils font des excursions ensemble.

Ils apprennent les bonnes manières, la politesse et le respect des valeurs morales aux enfants.

De mauvais parents:

Ils sont toujours en train de râler.

Ils partent souvent en vacances sans leurs enfants.

Ils sont très sévères.

Ils laissent leurs enfants tout faire.

Ils battent leurs enfants.

Ils gâtent leurs enfants.

Transcript 6 (see page 20)

Stéphanie

A mon avis mes parents sont les parents idéaux car ils sont drôles, gentils et généreux. Ils respectent beaucoup ma vie privée et m'encouragent dans les moments difficiles.

Christophe

Pour moi, de bons parents devraient faire preuve de confiance, de patience et d'amour. Ils devraient être justes sans jamais être méchants.

Thomas

Selon moi, les parents idéaux doivent traiter leurs enfants de façon égale. Ils doivent leur donner de bons conseils et apporter le soutien et l'amour dont tous les enfants ont besoin.

Transcript 7 (see page 21)

A mon avis pour être bon parent, on doit …

Selon moi, les parents idéaux devraient …

Je trouve que de bons parents devraient …

A mon avis un bon parent est quelqu'un qui …

Selon moi, les parents idéaux sont …

Transcript 8 (see page 21)

… parce que ça apprend aux enfants à être plus polis

… car ça aide les enfants à mieux travailler à l'école

… ça rend les enfants plus indépendants et les prépare pour l'avenir

… ça apprend aux enfants à mieux communiquer avec d'autres personnes.

TOPIC 4 **Holidays with or without Parents? – Les Vacances avec ou sans Parents?**

Transcript 9 (see page 22)

Les avantages

Ils nous payent tout ce que nous voulons.

On se sent plus en sécurité.

On peut faire des excursions ensemble.

Ils nous amènent au restaurant.

Ils s'occupent de nous.

Ils portent les valises.

Ils s'occupent de tous les papiers.

Les inconvénients

Ils ne s'amusent pas de la même façon.

Ils ne nous laissent rien faire tous seuls.

Il faut tout le temps aller avec eux.

On n'aime pas les mêmes choses.

Il faut toujours demander la permission si on veut sortir en boîte.

On se dispute plus souvent.

Ils peuvent être humiliants.

Transcript 10 (see page 22)

Je vais vous parler des avantages et des inconvénients de partir en vacances avec ses parents.

Je vais vous parler des avantages et des inconvénients qu'il y a à partir en vacances en famille.

Je vais vous expliquer pourquoi je préfère partir en vacances avec mes parents au lieu de mes amis.

Je pars toujours en vacances avec mes parents et je vais vous expliquer les avantages de ce genre de voyage.

Selon moi, il y a beaucoup d'avantages et d'inconvénients de partir en vacances en famille/avec ses parents.

TOPIC 5 Ideal Holidays/Tourism – Les Vacances Idéales/Le Tourisme

Transcript 11 (see page 24)

Julien – Quelles seraient tes vacances idéales?

Mon rêve serait d'aller au Mexique pour faire de la planche à voile et découvrir un pays différent du mien. J'irais probablement avec mon frère car on s'entend très bien ensemble et je sais qu'on s'amuserait comme des fous. On irait là-bas pour un mois et on passerait les deux premières semaines sur la plage et puis on irait visiter le Mexique profond.

Sylvie – Où aimerais-tu le plus passer tes vacances et pourquoi?

Oh, moi c'est sûr que j'irais à Rome parce que j'adore la culture italienne et je trouve que Rome est une des plus belles villes du monde. On irait au mois de mai car il y aurait moins de touristes et il ne ferait pas trop chaud. On est une famille assez religieuse alors j'irais sans doute avec toute ma famille pour voir le Pape et aller à la messe dans la basilique St-Pierre. On visiterait tous les plus beaux quartiers de Rome et on mangerait tous les soirs dans de bons restaurants. J'adore la cuisine italienne alors j'y serais vraiment heureuse.

Farid – Où aimerais-tu te rendre pour les vacances?

J'aimerais visiter l'Irlande parce que j'aimerais y découvrir de beaux paysages et apprendre plus sur les traditions de ce merveilleux pays. J'irais sans doute au mois de juin car il y pleut sûrement moins. Du moins, je l'espère. Pendant mon séjour que je ferais seul, je ferais des randonnées en vélo en m'arrêtant dans chaque pub irlandais pour y écouter de la musique traditionnelle en buvant une pinte de Guiness.

Christine – Quelles seraient tes vacances idéales?

Moi, j'aimerais aller en Australie en hiver parce que j'aimerais trop passer Noël et le jour de l'an sur la plage et faire un barbecue. J'irais avec ma meilleure amie et on irait découvrir le 'Outback', voir la Barrière de Corail et aller sur la plage pour regarder de beaux australiens faire du surf. J'aimerais aussi visiter Sydney où j'achèterais plein de cadeaux pour toute ma famille. Ce genre de voyage m'aiderait aussi à améliorer mon anglais que j'étudie à la fac en ce moment.

TOPIC 6 Home Area – Chez Soi

Transcript 12 – Living in town (see page 27)

Il y a beaucoup de choses à faire et à voir.

Il y a beaucoup de voitures et par conséquent trop de pollution.

La vie en ville peut être stressante à cause du bruit et de la circulation.

Il n'y a pas assez d'espaces verts.

Il y a trop de monde en ville et par conséquent on est toujours stressé.

Il y a énormément de divertissements à proximité.

On n'est pas obligé d'avoir une voiture car il y a de bons transports en commun.

Les loyers en ville sont très élevés et c'est donc très difficile de trouver un appartement convenable.

On peut se sentir seul car il y a un fort anonymat en ville.

Il y a beaucoup de crime en ville et donc on ne se sent pas toujours en sécurité.

Transcript 13 – Living in the country (see page 28)

Il y a peu de possibilités de travail, alors beaucoup de jeunes quittent la campagne pour aller chercher du travail en ville.

Tout le monde connaît ses voisins alors on ne se sent jamais seul.

C'est très agréable pour les enfants parce que les parents peuvent les laisser jouer dehors sans s'inquiéter.

Il n'y a rien aux alentours et on s'ennuie facilement.

On peut profiter de la nature et de la tranquillité.

Les gens sont moins stressés à la campagne et on arrive à mieux se détendre.

Il n'y a pas beaucoup de circulation et par conséquent peu de bruit et de pollution.

Tout le monde est toujours au courant de tout ce qu'on fait ce qui peut parfois être gênant.

L'air est pur et on peut se promener tranquillement dans les champs sans se sentir étouffé par le bruit et la saleté en ville.

La campagne n'est pas bien desservie par les transports en commun et il faut donc souvent avoir une voiture pour se déplacer.

Transcript 14 – Living by the sea (see page 28)

On se sent toujours en vacances parce que la plage est à proximité.

Les voitures sont vite rouillées à cause de l'air marin.

Les odeurs de poisson et de la mer peuvent parfois être désagréables.

Lorsqu'il fait beau on peut passer ses journées à la plage sans dépenser d'argent.

Il y a toujours beaucoup de travail en été pour les étudiants.

Il y a souvent du brouillard ce qui peut être très dangereux pour conduire.

Le paysage est vraiment beau malgré le temps.

On peut faire beaucoup de sports aquatiques ce qui est vraiment super.

Le bruit de la mer est très paisible et aide à se détendre.

En hiver la mer est souvent très agitée et ça peut être très dangereux.

En été il y a beaucoup de touristes et les résidents de la ville se plaignent des encombrements qu'ils provoquent.

Transcript 15 – (see pages 28 to 29)

A mon avis la vie en ville est agréable parce que ...

J'adore vivre en ville car ...

Selon moi, la vie en ville n'est pas très agréable car ...

Les inconvénients de vivre en ville sont que ...

Il y a beaucoup d'avantages et d'inconvénients à vivre à la campagne. Les avantages sont que ...

Je trouve que vivre à la campagne est mieux que de vivre en ville parce que ...

Je n'aime pas vivre à la campagne parce que ...

Les raisons pour lesquelles j'adore vivre au bord de la mer sont que ...

Transcript 16 – Where you would like to live (see page 29)

J'aimerais mieux vivre en ville/à la campagne/au bord de la mer parce que ...

Quand je quitterai l'école, je voudrais vivre en ville, parce que ...

J'ai toujours rêvé de vivre au bord de la mer, parce que ...

Quand je serai plus vieux (vieille) j'aimerais vivre en ville, car ...

Transcript 17 – Where you wouldn't like to live (see page 29)

Je ne pourrais jamais vivre en ville, car ...

Je ne quitterais jamais la ville pour vivre à la campagne parce que ...

Je ne serais pas heureux(se) si je vivais à la campagne car ...

Je n'aimerais pas habiter en ville, parce que ...

TOPIC 7 Leisure and Healthy Living – Les Loisirs et La Santé

Transcript 18 (see page 32)

1 Pour être en bonne santé, il faut manger beaucoup de fruits et de légumes et faire un peu de sport.

2 Pour se maintenir en forme, on doit manger équilibré et faire du sport, comme jouer au foot ou faire de la natation.

3 Pour garder la ligne, il faut surtout boire beaucoup d'eau, manger sainement et faire de l'exercice.

4 Ce qui est bon pour la santé, c'est de manger à des heures régulières et d'avoir une alimentation riche en vitamine.

5 A mon avis le secret d'une bonne santé, c'est de faire du sport tous les jours et de manger ce dont on a envie.

Transcript 19 (see page 33)

Les gens fument/boivent trop d'alcool/prennent de la drogue ...
... pour échapper à la réalité
... pour avoir l'air cool
... pour oublier les problèmes familiaux
... par souci d'appartenance à un groupe social
... parce qu'ils sont influencés par les amis
... à cause du stress de la société
... pour perdre du poids
... pour faire comme les autres/les amis/les parents
... pour le plaisir.

Transcript 20 (see page 34)

The Effects of Smoking – Les Effets de La Cigarette

La nicotine est très néfaste pour notre système sanguin.
Elle nuit au corps et à la santé.

La fumée est nocive pour le fumeur ainsi que le non-fumeur.
La fumée pique les yeux et pollue l'air ambiant.

La cigarette est responsable de grave maladies comme ...
  ... l'asthme
  ... les troubles cardiaques
  ... le cancer.
La cigarette rend la peau grise et la fait vieillir prématurément.

La cigarette donne mauvaise haleine et jaunit les dents.
Les fumeurs ont souvent les doigts jaunes.

Transcript 21 (see page 35)

The Effects of Alcohol – Les Effets de L'Alcool

L'alcool n'a pas une grande valeur nutritionnelle et peut faire grossir.
L'alcool donne mauvaise haleine.
Consommer de l'alcool de manière irresponsable peut être dangereux pour soi ainsi que pour ses proches.

L'alcool affecte le cerveau et affaiblit nos facultés physiques et mentales.
On ne sait plus ce qu'on fait lorsqu'on boit trop d'alcool.
Trop d'alcool rend souvent les gens violents.

Trop d'alcool peut provoquer de graves maladies comme ...
  ... les maladies cardio-vasculaires
  ... le cancer du foie.

Transcript 22 (see page 36)

The Effects of Drug Use – Les Effets de La Drogue

La drogue affecte les réflexes.
Elle est très dangereuse pour le cerveau et le système sanguin.
La prise de drogue peut engendrer de graves maladies.

La drogue peut coûter cher.
La drogue et la criminalité sont souvent liées.

Certaines drogues conduisent à la dépendance.
La drogue peut faire de l'homme une épave.
A un certain stade il devient difficile de s'en passer.

La drogue affecte le comportement social.
La vie normale s'écroule.
Ça mène parfois à la solitude.

Transcript 23 (see page 37)

Pour décourager/dissuader les jeunes de prendre ces substances abusives ...

Il faut augmenter les campagnes publicitaires exposant les dangers de la drogue/de la cigarette/de l'alcool.

Il faut encourager les parents et l'école à leur parler de ses dangers aussitôt que possible.

On doit en parler ouvertement et insister sur les effets néfastes de la drogue/de la cigarette/de l'alcool.

On doit interdire les affiches publicitaires.

Transcript 24 (see page 38)

I. Bonjour Julien, aujourd'hui nous allons parler de la santé. Quels sont tes avis sur ce sujet?

J. A mon avis il est très important de rester en bonne santé pour vivre le plus longtemps possible. Il faut un régime équilibré, faire de l'exercice et essayer d'éviter les drogues comme la cigarette et l'alcool.

I. Alors que fais-tu pour rester en bonne santé?

J. En général, je mange une nourriture très saine avec beaucoup de produits frais comme des légumes et des fruits. Je mange peu de matière grasse mais j'ai une faiblesse pour les sucreries et parfois, quand je suis triste, je me gave de chocolat et de bonbons. Je sais qu'il ne faut pas trop en manger car c'est mauvais pour les dents mais ça ne peut pas faire de mal de temps en temps.

I. Fais-tu du sport pour rester en forme?

J. Malheureusement je n'aime pas trop le sport mais je m'efforce d'aller à la piscine deux fois par semaine pour faire de la natation.

I. Julien, quels sont tes avis sur les substances nocives comme la cigarette, la drogue et l'alcool?

J. De nos jours les gens ont un souci d'appartenance sociale qui les pousse à consommer ces produits. Au début ils croient qu'ils ont l'air cool mais avant qu'ils ne s'en rendent compte ils sont déjà dépendants de ces substances et les effets sont parfois très graves. Mon grand-père, par exemple, a fumé toute sa vie et est mort l'an dernier d'un cancer du poumon à l'âge de 71 ans.

I. Alors crois-tu qu'on peut faire quelque chose pour dissuader les gens de commencer à prendre ces substances?

J. A mon avis, on devrait mieux renseigner aux jeunes les effets de ces substances le plus tôt possible. Par exemple à l'école, dans les clubs des jeunes et même à la télé.

I. Merci Julien. As-tu autre chose à ajouter?

J. Oui, pour finir je dirais que si on peut manger sainement et faire un peu de sport tout en évitant de prendre des produits dangereux, on aura une qualité de vie meilleure et on vivra plus heureux et plus longtemps.

Transcript 25 (see page 38)

Je vais vous donner mes opinions sur la façon de rester en bonne santé. D'abord je parlerai de ce qu'il faut manger et faire pour se tenir en forme. Ensuite je vous donnerai mes avis sur les substances nocives comme la drogue et l'alcool.

Je vais vous expliquer comment, selon moi, on peut se maintenir en forme. Je commencerai par la nourriture et le sport. Puis je donnerai mes avis sur la drogue/l'alcool et la cigarette et leurs effets sur notre corps.

Transcript 26 (see page 39)

Pour conclure, je pense que pour se tenir en forme on doit d'abord se sentir bien dans sa peau et éviter toutes les substances qui abusent notre corps.

Pour finir, je dirais que pour rester en bonne santé il faut avoir une alimentation variée et faire un peu de sport. On doit boire avec modération et ne prendre ni drogue ni cigarette.

TOPIC 8 Television and Films – La Télévision et Les Films

Transcript 27 (see page 41)

Regardes-tu souvent la télé?

1 Non, je la regarde rarement.

2 Oui, je la regarde assez souvent.

3 Je la regarde de temps en temps quand il y a quelque chose d'intéressant.

4 En général non, mais pendant les vacances je la regarde pendant des heures.

5 Je regarde la télé quand je m'ennuie ce qui ne m'arrive guère.

Transcript 28 (see page 41)

1 Je n'aime regarder que les informations à la télé car ça me permet d'être au courant des événements mondiaux.

2 J'adore les dessins animés parce qu'ils sont très marrants et nous aident à sortir de la routine journalière.

3 J'aime beaucoup regarder les émissions de sport surtout l'athlétisme. Je fais beaucoup de sport et voir le professionnalisme de ces gens me motive plus.

Transcript 29 (see page 41)

1 Je déteste les feuilletons à la télé et je ne les regarde jamais. Dès qu'on commence à les regarder, on ne peut plus s'arrêter. C'est vraiment comme une drogue.

2 J'ai vraiment du mal à regarder les documentaires biographiques. Je les trouve peu intéressants et parfois un peu embarrassants.

3 Je déteste les émissions comiques car je ne les trouve absolument pas drôles. De plus, on est forcé d'écouter les faux rires d'une audience qui n'est même pas présente et honnêtement ça m'énerve beaucoup.

Transcript 30 (see page 42)

A mon avis, il y a plusieurs aspects positifs:

La télé est un bon moyen de ...
... découvrir de nouveaux horizons
... découvrir d'autres cultures
... se détendre (après l'école).

Il y a des émissions pour tous les goûts comme ...
... des dessins animés

... des feuilletons
... des émissions sportives
... des jeux
... des émissions de musique.

La télé nous apprend des choses sur ...
... d'autres pays
... la science
... la nature.

C'est un bon moyen de communication.
C'est un moyen de communication extraordinaire.

C'est éducatif:
La télé nous informe
    ... nous divertit
    ... nous enseigne
    ... nous instruit.

La télé joue un rôle culturel. Elle donne accès ...
... à la musique
... à la culture
... à l'histoire.

Transcript 31 (see page 43)

Malheureusement il y a plusieurs aspects négatifs comme:

On court le risque ...
... de devenir mollasson
... de devenir pantouflard.

Il y en a qui ne peuvent pas s'en passer.
Il y a trop de gens qui passent leur vie devant 'le petit écran'.

La télé ...
... nous abêtit
... nous ramollit
... nous rend fainéant.
La télé peut empêcher les gens de faire d'autre choses plus intéressantes.

La télé a tendance à briser la communication.
On ne parle plus à autrui.

Il y a trop ...
... de bêtises
... de jeux
... d'émissions idiotes
... d'émissions de qualité médiocre
... de dessins animés.
La télé est surchargée de publicité ridicule et inutile.

Certaines émissions sont idiotes/banales.
Il y a trop de feuilletons qui sont plus idiots les uns que les autres.
Certaines séries sont interminables.

Transcript 32 (see page 45)

Un bon prof est celui qui est ...
exemple,   sérieux
          patient
          prêt à aider
          consciencieux
          chaleureux
          équitable

Un bon prof est celui qui ...
exemple,   explique tout clairement
          apporte de l'aide nécessaire
          prépare bien ses cours

Un bon prof a ...
exemple,   le sens de l'humour

Un mauvais prof est celui ...
exemple,   qui n'est pas patient
          qui n'explique rien
          qui n'a pas le sens de l'humour

Un bon lycée est celui qui a ...
exemple,   une atmosphère sympa
          un bon taux de réussite aux examens
          de la discipline
          de bons rapports entre profs et élèves

Un bon lycée est celui où ...
exemple,   les élèves ont envie de réussir
          les profs sont disponibles
          il n'y a pas de violence

Un bon lycée est celui qui ...
exemple,   signale les absences
          protège ses élèves
          est bien équipé

Transcript 33 (see page 46)

I. Bonjour Julien. Aujourd'hui nous allons parler de l'école et des professeurs. A ton avis qu'est-ce qu'un bon prof?

J. Un bon prof, c'est une personne qui tout d'abord a un très bon sens de l'humour. Les élèves n'aiment pas un prof qui parle toujours devant sa classe sans jamais faire de blagues. Etre prof ne veut pas dire qu'il faut être sérieux et sévère.

I. C'est tout?

J. Non, certainement pas! Un bon prof doit présenter la matière qu'il enseigne de manière claire et précise. Il doit bien expliquer et donner beaucoup d'exemples avant de demander aux élèves de faire leurs travaux. Les élèves trouvent une matière plus facile lorsque le prof donne beaucoup d'exemples avant de faire une activité. Ils aiment bien aussi lorsqu'un prof prend le temps de venir leur expliquer personnellement des choses qu'ils ne comprennent pas. Un bon prof doit toujours être là pour aider ses élèves.

I. Quel est le pire défaut pour un prof?

J. Le pire défaut pour un prof est de ne pas être équitable. Si un prof a un chouchou dans la classe, il se fait détester par le reste des élèves. Un prof doit toujours aider ses élèves de façon égale. Il ne doit pas seulement travailler avec les élèves les plus forts.

I. Y a-t-il autre chose que les élèves détestent?

J. Oui, les élèves n'aiment pas vraiment les profs qui donnent trop de devoirs sans raisons. Il est nécessaire de donner des devoirs aux élèves, mais si on en donne trop, les élèves se fatiguent et n'aiment plus la matière enseignée.

I. Très bien. Et selon toi, Julien, qu'est-ce qu'une bonne école?

J. A mon avis, une bonne école est un endroit où les jeunes se sentent comme chez eux. Les élèves doivent éprouver un sentiment d'appartenance envers l'école qu'ils fréquentent. De plus une bonne école est un endroit où le personnel est chaleureux et enjoué. Si le personnel d'une école se comporte toujours comme s'il y avait quelqu'un de mort, les élèves ne s'y sentent pas bien. Tout le monde doit se sentir bienvenu et respecté.

I. Y a-t-il autre chose qui fait une bonne école?

J. Oui, l'école doit proposer plusieurs activités parascolaires intéressantes. Les élèves doivent sentir que l'école, ce n'est pas seulement les cours. Ils doivent pouvoir s'impliquer dans d'autres choses comme le sport, le théâtre, les voyages etc. Une bonne école doit proposer des activités variées pour intéresser tous types de personnalité.

TOPIC 2 School Uniform – L'Uniforme

Transcript 34 (see page 47)

Les avantages de porter un uniforme

Ça permet de distinguer les personnes ne faisant pas partie de l'école.

L'uniforme réduit les différences entre élèves.
On ne perd pas de temps à chercher comment on va s'habiller pour la journée.

On peut avoir une certaine fierté à porter un uniforme.

Ça a un certain chic et peut coûter moins cher que des vêtements de marque.

Ça nous distingue des autres écoles.
On se sent inclus dans un groupe social.

Porter un uniforme nous permet de mieux appréhender le monde du travail.

Transcript 35 (see page 48)

Les inconvénients de porter un uniforme

Ce n'est pas confortable pour travailler.
En été on a trop chaud et en hiver on a trop froid.

On perd son individualité.
On s'habille tous de la même façon.

Ce n'est pas pratique pour jouer.

Ça peut créer des conflits entre les écoles.

Ça nous oblige à acheter des vêtements qu'on n'aime pas forcément.

TOPIC 3 Subject Choice – Le Choix des Matières

Transcript 36 (see page 49)

Je m'intéresse beaucoup à la musique et donc j'ai décidé de l'étudier cette année.

J'ai décidé d'étudier le sport cette année car je suis très sportif(ve) et un jour j'aimerais être professeur de sport.

J'ai choisi l'informatique car je pense que de nos jours, il est très important de savoir bien maîtriser la technologie.

Je me passionne pour la lecture et la poésie alors j'ai choisi l'anglais pour approfondir mes connaissances.

J'ai choisi les maths cette année car je trouve que c'est indispensable pour la vie de tous les jours.

J'ai choisi les maths et la physique car je trouve que ce sont deux matières fondamentales pour mieux expliquer le monde qui nous entoure.

Transcript 37 (see page 49)

Je trouve que c'est très important d'étudier une langue étrangère car on devient plus tolérant envers d'autres cultures.

Le fait d'étudier une langue étrangère nous aide à mieux comprendre notre propre langue.

Une langue étrangère nous permet de communiquer avec les gens de différents pays.

J'ai choisi le français car je veux étudier les langues à la faculté.

A mon avis, les langues étrangères sont indispensables pour l'Union Européenne.

TOPIC 4 Future Aspirations – Aspirations Futures

Transcript 38 (see pages 53 to 54)

Go to university? – Aller à la faculté/à l'université?

Quand je quitterai l'école, j'aimerais aller à la fac pour étudier ... car je veux être ...

Si je réussis à mes examens, j'irai à l'université de Glasgow afin d'étudier le droit.

Go abroad? – Aller à l'étranger?

Un jour j'aimerais vivre à l'étranger car je m'intéresse beaucoup à d'autres cultures.

Quand je quitterai l'école, j'aimerais aller en France pour mieux connaître les traditions de ce pays et améliorer mon français.

A gap year? – Prendre une année sabbatique?

Quand je quitterai l'école, j'aimerais prendre une année sabbatique pour me reposer.

L'année prochaine, quand j'aurai quitté l'école, j'aimerais prendre une année sabbatique et faire du volontariat.

Look for a job? – Chercher du travail?

Après mon baccalauréat, j'aimerais commencer tout de suite à travailler pour gagner de l'argent.

Quand je quitterai l'école, j'aimerais trouver un travail car je veux mon propre appartement et mon indépendance.

Stay at home or leave? – Rester à la maison ou partir?

Je préférerais rester à la maison pendant mes études car on y a tout le confort pour étudier et ça me permettrait de dépenser moins d'argent.

J'aimerais aller à la fac dans une autre ville parce que je veux profiter de la vie d'étudiant.

Dès que je trouverai du travail, je déménagerai car je ne m'entends pas très bien avec mes parents.

Moi, je resterai à la maison le plus longtemps possible car je suis proche de ma famille et j'ai un peu peur de vivre loin d'elle.

Don't know? – Je ne sais pas?

Moi, je ne sais pas ce que je veux faire quand je quitterai l'école. D'ailleurs ça me fait un peu peur.

En ce moment je ne sais pas encore ce que je ferai lorsque je quitterai l'école mais ça ne m'inquiète pas trop.

Transcript 39 (see page 63)

L'an dernier je suis allé à Paris avec un groupe de vingt personnes.

Pendant les vacances de Noël je suis allé en France avec ma meilleure amie.

L'été dernier j'ai passé deux semaines en Bretagne avec l'école.

Pendant les vacances de Pâques, notre école a participé à un échange scolaire en France.

L'an dernier j'ai travaillé pendant un mois dans un hôtel à Toulouse dans le sud-ouest de la France.

Pendant les grandes vacances j'ai eu la chance de passer un mois à Lyon en France chez mon correspondant français.

Transcript 40 (see pages 65 to 66)

1 L'été dernier je suis allé en Bretagne dans le nord de la France avec l'école. Nous avons pris le car jusqu'à Douvres et puis le ferry jusqu'à Calais. Ensuite le car nous a amené jusqu'à notre destination en Bretagne. Le voyage était très long et ennuyeux et dans le ferry j'ai été malade. C'était vraiment affreux. Une fois arrivés, nous sommes allés à l'auberge de jeunesse qui se trouvait dans un petit village. Elle était vieille mais vraiment jolie. En plus je devais partager la chambre avec mon meilleur ami. C'était génial et on s'est bien amusé.

2 Pendant les vacances de Pâques, j'ai eu la chance de trouver un travail dans un hôtel à Paris en France. J'ai pris l'avion à l'aéroport de Glasgow le samedi matin et je suis arrivé à Paris à midi. Le voyage était super et très amusant car c'était la première fois que je prenais l'avion. Une fois arrivé à Paris, j'ai pris le métro pour aller dans le seizième arrondissement où se trouvait mon hôtel. Le métro n'était pas cher mais il était très sale. J'avais un peu peur. L'hôtel, par contre, était très propre et moderne. Il était vraiment pratique car il se trouvait à cinq minutes de la Tour Eiffel. C'était super. J'avais ma propre chambre qui était vraiment grande et très bien équipée. Je me suis senti tout de suite à l'aise.

3 Il y a un an, pendant les vacances de Noël, j'ai participé à un échange scolaire. Nous sommes allés à Grenoble dans les Alpes pour une semaine et c'était vraiment magnifique. On est parti de Glasgow en train le dimanche matin pour arriver à Grenoble le lundi à midi. Le voyage était ennuyeux car c'était très long et il faisait froid dans les wagons. A la gare de Grenoble les familles d'accueil nous attendaient pour nous amener chez elles. C'était très sympa de leur part. La maison de ma famille d'accueil était super. C'était comme un chalet suisse et il y avait une belle vue sur les Alpes. C'était très joli. La maison était spacieuse et moderne et j'avais même une chambre à moi.

4 Pendant les grandes vacances je suis allée en Provence, en France avec l'école. Nous étions vingt élèves et trois professeurs. Nous avons quitté Glasgow en car à une heure du matin et puis nous avons pris l'Eurostar pour arriver en France le lendemain à deux heures de l'après-midi. Ensuite on a continué notre voyage en car jusqu'à notre destination en Provence. Le voyage ne m'a pas semblé très long parce que le car était très confortable et qu'on a pu dormir. L'Eurostar était très pratique aussi. Nous avons logé dans une auberge de jeunesse en Provence qui se trouvait en pleine campagne. L'auberge était très vieille et assez sale. En plus les chambres étaient très petites et peu confortables. On n'était pas très content de notre logement.

Transcript 41 (see page 73)

L'été dernier je suis allée en Bretagne en France avec l'école. On y est resté une semaine et on a logé dans une auberge de jeunesse qui se trouvait à deux cents mètres de la plage. C'était super. Les jours de soleil on passait beaucoup de temps sur la plage à jouer au volley-ball et à se baigner. On a même rencontré de beaux garçons français. Ils étaient vraiment sympa. On a aussi fait quelques excursions pour visiter la région. Le soir on mangeait au restaurant. La nourriture était vraiment bonne. Les spécialités de la Bretagne sont le poisson et les fruits de mer et j'ai pu en manger tous les jours.

L'an dernier pendant les vacances de Pâques je suis allé à Lyon dans l'est de la France. J'y ai travaillé comme serveur dans un grand hôtel pendant un mois et j'ai eu ma propre chambre dans l'hôtel. Quand je ne travaillais pas je faisais de belles promenades dans la vieille ville. L'architecture lyonnaise est vraiment belle et j'ai pu prendre beaucoup de jolies photos. Le soir j'allais soit en boîte de nuit avec mes collègues soit (on sortait) boire un verre dans un café. Comme je ne gagnais pas beaucoup d'argent, j'ai dû manger à la cantine du personnel de l'hôtel. La nourriture n'était vraiment pas bonne à l'hôtel. On mangeait toujours la même chose et c'était trop gras ou trop froid.

Il y a quatre semaines je suis allé avec mes parents pour un week-end dans les Alpes en France. On a loué un chalet avec deux chambres avec vue sur les pistes. C'était magnifique. Le samedi nous avons fait du ski et du snow-board. Le dimanche matin nous sommes restés à l'hôtel car il neigeait fort et donc on ne pouvait pas sortir. A midi on a mangé une raclette qui est une des spécialités de la région. C'était vraiment délicieux. Le dimanche après-midi on a pu sortir et aller dans la petite ville pour acheter des cadeaux pour nos amis en Ecosse. J'ai passé un week-end inoubliable mais c'était un peu court.